Living *with* Momma

Living *with* Momma

*A Good Person's Guide
to Caring for Aging Parents,
Adult Children, and Ourselves*

Elizabeth B. Adams, MAPT

NASHVILLE

NEW YORK • LONDON • MELBOURNE • VANCOUVER

Living *with* Momma
A Good Person's Guide to Caring for Aging Parents,
Adult Children, and Ourselves

© 2019 Elizabeth B. Adams, MAPT

Published in New York, New York, by Morgan James Publishing in partnership with Difference Press. Morgan James is a trademark of Morgan James, LLC. www.MorganJamesPublishing.com

The Morgan James Speakers Group can bring authors to your live event. For more information or to book an event visit The Morgan James Speakers Group at www.TheMorganJamesSpeakersGroup.com.

ISBN 978-1-64279-147-1 paperback
ISBN 978-1-64279-148-8 eBook
Library of Congress Control Number: 2018907293

In an effort to support local communities, raise awareness and funds, Morgan James Publishing donates a percentage of all book sales for the life of each book to Habitat for Humanity Peninsula and Greater Williamsburg.

Get involved today! Visit
www.MorganJamesBuilds.com

*For the boy who asked me to prom
and the man I have loved dancing with
for over thirty-seven years.*

Table of Contents

Foreword

By Rosemary Daniell

When I first met Elizabeth Adams at a Zona Rosa writing retreat I was leading for women in the North Georgia mountains, I was struck by her beautiful, loving demeanor. At the time, I was under a great deal of stress, seeking to help one of my adult daughter's out of a difficult life situation that, despite my efforts, seemed to be escalating instead of getting better.

That first night, as Elizabeth and I sat on the couch in the relaxing living room of the ranch where we would spend the next two days, we talked and she immediately—as though she sensed what was going on—shared that she too had had a family situation that was disruptive to her peace of mind. At the same time, she seemed calm, as though neither that difficulty, nor the stresses of her various professions—adoption advocate and pastoral counselor to parents of sick children among them—had fractured her serenity in the way my situation had mine.

All weekend too, I observed her grace and supportiveness of the other women writers in our group as we discussed their writing projects. It was Mother's Day weekend, and I noticed that—while I was spending my time after our sessions making frantic phone calls home, seeking to resolve the latest crisis, Elizabeth was on her smart phone—with her adult children—looking relaxed and delighted to hear from them.

During those moments, I knew I wanted what she had.

Flash forward a month during which the problems in my daughter's life—and thus, my own life, accelerated at an even more rapid pace, making me feel as though I was being swept up in vortex. While my daughter's long-standing opioid addiction appeared to be under control, these crises were magnified by the fact that she had also become physically disabled as the result of a series of falls. At one point, after accompanying her to doctor appointment after doctor appointment, I had pushed myself to fulfill her every need as she first moved in with me to escape an abusive boyfriend, then back to her apartment after I'd cleaned and packed her belongings in an effort to create a calm environment for her when she returned. The next day, after moving her back in, I'd shopped for groceries for her, and delivered them, knowing full well I had to drive five plus hours through heavy traffic to Atlanta early the next morning to lead a Zona Rosa workshop there. Instead, I found myself on a desolate exit ramp off of a busy freeway, seeking to calm myself in the midst of a terrifying panic attack.

Back at home—not having made it to Atlanta—I realized I had no choice. If I wanted to remain sane and productive, I had to change. That night, I made a list, enumerating what I would and would not do (mostly, *not*) to achieve this goal—a goal that didn't mean I loved my daughter any less, but only that I had to also begin love myself more. As I read it to my husband, I saw the relief in his eyes. While I had been concerned for her, he had been concerned for *me*, often saying he was worried that I'd still be doing this in my 80's, a birthday I had recently reached.

Besides seeking to save my daughter's life during the many active years of her addiction, I had also care-given my husband after a near fatal heart attack, a subsequent staph infection and a years-long bout with alcoholism. Along the way, I had become guardian to my schizophrenic adult son, taking him to doctor's appointments, seeing that he was properly housed and caregiving him in my home until his death from cancer. As payee for both he and his sister's disability checks, I was also responsible for their finances, and thus needs—all the while seeking to make a life for myself as a writer and teacher.

Once, during all this, I'd bought a book, *How to Change Your Life and Everyone in It in One Month or Less*, and tried over and over to follow its instructions. But now, despite the problem-solving, "can do" nature that I'd always prided myself on, and however beloved others might be to me, I was ready to face the fact that there might be limits to what I could do, and that this time, I might need a more spiritual approach.

Thus, when Elizabeth emailed me, asking me to read her book, *Living with Momma*, and possibly write the foreword for it, I felt blessed—that the heavens had, with perfect synchronicity, dropped a gift into my life. Indeed, I was hungry and in need of whatever wisdom she had to share. As a Zen proverb says, "When the student is ready, the teacher will appear." And as I began reading, I knew beyond a doubt I was about to learn exactly what I needed to know.

It turned out that Elizabeth, too, had her own wake up call, though hers had to do with seeking to care-give her beloved mother, Bobbi, who was terminally ill with cancer three hundred miles away. Like me, she had sought to do more that than she could comfortably do (her story, like the stories of many other women, is detailed in the book, so I won't give it away here), leading her too, to a dangerous situation on a long drive on a freeway.

The first and most striking thing I learned as I read is what Elizabeth describes as the difference between caretaking—that is, doing things for others—and caregiving, which is caring for them from the heart. Yes, I loved my daughter, but I wasn't doing her any favors by hurting myself and my serenity, and the idea of coming from love—loving myself as I loved her—came as a huge relief.

Elizabeth, who describes herself as a "practical theologian" is exactly that. Throughout *Living with Momma*, she deals with true life situations, and gives us down-to-earth, usable advice at the same time that—as a Navajo saying goes—she "speaks to the highest that is in us." Calling on the wisdom of the ages, she asks us to answer three life-changing—and surprising—questions, which you'll find early on in the book. She suggests we begin a reflective journal, stopping to contemplate inspiring Biblical readings as we do so. She helps us to learn to say "I need…," a phrase that comes hard to some of us. At this point, my daughter was at the stage, described in a *New Yorker* cartoon, in which one woman tells another, "I'm at that point in life when I don't want my parents to tell me what to do but I still want to blame them for it." The day I was able to journal that I had actually said "I don't want to" in response to one of her "urgent" requests was a huge breakthrough.

As Elizabeth emphasizes, we don't have "to do" things to be a loving person. And yes, protecting our *own* peace is imperative. She suggests that we use silence, solitude, meditative prayer and reflective listening to avoid caretaker burnout. Further along, she gives us simple instructions for more effective, loving communications with family members, and as importantly, with ourselves. "The problem comes when we forget to love ourselves along with others," she asserts, referring to the Bible verse that asks us to love others as we love *our*selves.

Calling the generation for whom she writes the "sandwich clan," she cites the statistics that tell us that 4 out of 10 Americans care for family members with health issues related to aging, and more adult children are living in their parents' homes than anytime since the 1950s, despite that society today frowns on this practice. As I read, I recalled my own family: the great grandparents who lived with my grandparents until they passed away, my distant cousin Myrtie or "Cudden" as we called them back then—who went to work downtown in Atlanta each day to support herself, her bedridden sister Cudden Lily, and her brother, Cudden Grover even though he was, in the Southern vernacular, "no good," meaning he went fishing everyday instead of working. When we visited the terminally ill among us, it was just as often in their own homes as in a hospital. My destitute alcoholic father lived with his mother, my paternal grandmother, until she died and he suddenly and mysteriously quit drinking. And all this was done without question, and even with love, and the sense that every person, no matter how strange, was of value, just as in the anthropological examples Elizabeth gives of our very human desire to take care of "the least among us."

In my experience, few little girls grow up thinking—beyond daydreaming about caring for their own adorable and problem-free young children—that she wants to take care of others—adult others— for a large part of her life. Like most, and maybe more than most, I dreamed of romance and adventure and didn't even take good care of my dolls, tearing them up and carrying around only their heads. Like most women, we hadn't seen it coming. But then my sister and I learned early about the problems adults could have when our dashing father lost his job because of drink, and our beautiful but anxious mother went to work to support us even as she sank deeper and deeper into the depression that would eventually lead to her suicide. Yet despite—or perhaps because— of this, I became a control freak, still believing that, fueled by my pride, my blind ambition, I could control not only my destiny, but that of my three beloved children by giving them childhoods totally different from my own. Along the way, I chose to ignore the fact that they had three alcoholic grandparents and a bipolar grandmother; also that my maternal grandmother had, like I would later have, a bipolar, addicted daughter and schizophrenic son. (Not surprisingly, my older daughter, their sister, is now a psychiatrist, ministering to the severely mentally ill and the marginalized.)

In addition, over the 37 years I've led Zona Rosa writing workshops, which have been attended by thousands of women (and some men), I've learned that too many of them to enumerate here have served, or were serving as caregivers to loved ones. In a recent group, only one woman had not had one or more extended caretaking/caregiving experiences, and she was an only child who had never lived with another person, married or had children. Two who were nurses (one my sister) said that their career choices had nothing to do with the desire to care take— nursing had simply seemed to be the best choice available to them at the time, but that later caregiving had become natural to them. Among the others, Courtney left grad school, giving up a prestigious fellowship in art history to go home and care—for the next 20 years until his death from cancer—for her schizophrenic son. Claudia tended her dying mother, then her terminally ill husband, and recently, her schizoaffective-disordered son until his death in a state-run crisis center. Despite her career as a chemist, and the fact that her husband was in a wheelchair with multiple sclerosis, Vaiju took in his mother until her death from Alzheimer's, and later his just-out-of-jail, jobless brother until his death from cancer. And Carolyn had cared for her husband during a terminal bout with ALS, or Lou Gehrig's disease. And on and on in what could be a book in itself.

For such women—and men, for they are often caregivers, too— Elizabeth Adams' *Living with Momma: A Good Person's Guide to Caring for Aging Parents, Adult Children, and Ourselves* will serve an inspiring guide to what, for most of us, becomes one of life's inevitabilities. Both practical and spiritual in approach, Elizabeth's uniquely refreshing perspective can lead us to wholeness and a less divided life, all the while acknowledging the love that lies behind our actions in the first place. As I turned the last page, I was immensely grateful to her, and I'm certain that her many readers will close this invaluable book feeling the same way.

Rosemary Daniell's recently completed third memoir is *My Beautiful Tigers: Forty Years as the Mother of an Opioid Addicted Daughter and a Schizophrenic Son.* She is the author of *Secrets of the Zona Rosa: How Writing (and Sisterhood) Can Change Women's Lives* and *The Woman Who Spilled Words All Over Herself,* as well six other books of poetry and prose. Early in her career, as part of the National Endowment for the Arts Poetry in the Schools program, she instigated and led writing workshops in women's prisons in Georgia and Wyoming. In 2008, she received a Governor's Award in the Humanities for her impact on the state of Georgia. She is profiled in the book *Feminists Who Changed America, 1963-1975.*

Introduction

Susan, age fifty-four, sat nervously twisting well-used tissues as she attempted to talk to me between all the tears. She was stressed out. She had every reason to be with all the responsibilities she had taken on over the past couple of years. She could not understand how, after working hard and "doing all the right things," that her life could be so out of control.

Susan's adult children had moved back into her home again. Her company was facing a downsizing situation. Although mother's cancer was finally in remission, she still needed to chauffeur her to physical therapy after breaking her foot last month. Susan could not afford to miss any work with her company drama swirling around her, and this made the weekly therapy appointments hard to come by, which meant her mother was mad at her for not being more willing to help.

Susan believed she had spent most of her life "making things work out for her family." Lately, she woke each day in a bad mood and went to bed every night too tired to sleep. When I approached Susan, she wanted to talk about how someone with her non-stop and ever-growing schedule could ever return to enjoying life again. Was this how life was supposed to be? Should she "get used to the fact that these are some disappointing times, and just get over herself?"

Susan, like millions of Americans, was taking care of an aging parent and adult children at the same time. Today, four out of ten Americans care for an adult family member with health issues related to aging. According to the U.S. Census Bureau, more adult children (age thirty-five and younger) are living in their parents' homes than at any time since the 1880s. This situation only added to her everyday stress of juggling a job, a home, and a family.

I started researching this family dynamic shift in 2011, and I tell people in similar situations about these staggering numbers because I hope they will see that they are not alone. When this multi-generational family shift occurred in my family, I never saw it coming; most people I speak with do not see it coming in their lives either. Forewarned is forearmed, so to speak.

Like Susan, the majority of people I speak with are hardworking and have found themselves in very complicated lives. They are good people who have taken on the responsibility of being a caretaker for the seemingly urgent needs of those they love most. This position, of being sandwiched between the older (baby boomer) and younger (millennial and Gen Xer) generations, is further complicated because it happens right smack in the middle of life—*middle age*—when we typically tend to question issues of self-worth and identity.

Questioning our self-worth and identity is a riptide in reality. We see that what we expected to happen by this time has not and, at the midlife milestone, those expectations are unlikely to be realized. Even without the stress of becoming a primary caregiver for an aging parent or navigating a healthy relationship with an adult child, middle age is a time in life when divorce rates peak and major career changes are made.

Around 2007, I too, was captured by the "clan of the sandwich generation." The term sandwich generation is used for the people who are attempting to live in the space between adult children and aging parents. Consciously or not, this life event sneaks up on you when you are distracted: the children are (finally) ready to leave the nest and your parents are retiring, preferably to a condo in Florida so you have a free place to stay near the beach. At least that is what I remembered being told would happen around middle age. Don't all the movies, TV shows, and books about becoming empty nesters tell us that we will no longer have to stretch ourselves so thin when we hit this point in our lives? Did we miss the memo that said it's time to take a break as a reward for a job well done?

It has been said "it is easy to give advice, but it is hard to tell your story." That was where I was: I was a professional caregiver who needed help myself. I started looking for people who not only were wise members of the sandwich generation but also had the special skills of being compassionate listeners. People who asked open-ended questions and offered secure spaces or as my favorite spiritual teacher Parker J. Palmer suggests, a place "to hear my soul speak" because "the soul is shy and needs a safe place" to show itself. I searched for people with soulful qualities who were open to telling me their stories of living with aging parents and adult children. My own shy, discouraged, lonely soul needed to glean some courage from the eternally good stories of my sandwich clan.

As a practical theologian, I also knew there were sacred texts to learn from. I just needed to discover where to find them. As the old saying goes, "a toothbrush won't help you at all unless you put it in your mouth and apply it to your teeth," and that's all practical theology is—a useful tool like a toothbrush.

Even though I have a master's in theology, when it comes to spirituality I am absolutely sure of only two ideas: (1) we are all created in the image of an unconditionally Loving Creator; and (2) the soul that a perfect-loving Universal Creator breathed into us must be paid attention to.

The point of this book is to remind you of the importance of paying attention to your true self, your caring essence, your life-giving spiritual selves.

These reminders come in the form of practical theology. You will apply spiritual truths to your lives by doing actions (or suggested exercises) to remember that you already have what you need as a "good" person taking care of your aging parents and adult children: increasing amounts of love, joy, peace, patience, kindness, goodness, gentleness, and self-control (Eph. 5:22–23). These are given as gifts to your famished soul. They are promises from the Creator. They are gifts of the Holy Spirit. They are spaces where your humanity and your divinity meet and walk in the "cool of the garden" together.

Each chapter in this book introduces a question or a mantra and tells stories of people who are seeking answers while being good caregivers. Each chapter also offers a broader guide to growing valuable resources for our essential caring selves during daily interactions with family members. It is there that we see the beautiful impact multi-generational living can have on our society. These are open spaces that remind us that love should never be regulated or seen conditionally as having "a right way." Whereas no book could include every issue the twenty-first century hands us, concerning our families, this book suggests many ways we can go further and deeper in our own fruitful journeys toward securing rewarding relationships.

We will explore stories shared by people who are living with aging parents and adult children. Most of the characters and details in these stories are compilations of real-life narratives and people I have worked with, anonymized for privacy. Some stories include multiple perspectives because I was blessed with more than one member in a family who wanted to talk about their multi-generational lifestyle. Bottom line, these stories allow you to see that when good people are in hard situations, learning some basics in practical theology can help ease the way forward for anyone.

Chapters 1 and 2 guide you to ask two questions that open a safe space for your essential self to emerge. They introduce the concept of *LIVING* within a context of family drama and then offer a way for you to retell your story to have an immediate and radical calming effect on intense everyday situations.

Chapters 3, 4, and 5 introduce people who are *LIVING* with the gifts of being a caregiver in the foreground of their choices. They offer examples of the fruits of the Spirit (Eph. 5:22–23) that can feed famished souls and virtues that can welcome peace into your heart. Each story shows how healing, choices, acceptance, or a view of the larger picture have transformed individual and group experiences.

Chapters 6 and 7 introduce people who are *LIVING* with some of the hard decisions you must make as a caregiver. Again, stories can uncover the mistakes you cannot see until you learn to live in sync with your essential caring self. Using the paths other people are walking will guide you through the emotional terrains of sharing space and resources to nourish everyone in your family and yourself.

Chapters 8 and 9 guide you to begin applying practical theology to your human and spiritual self as you make the hard decisions about redefining priorities, and becoming stronger and more whole by rewriting your family stories with your own life.

Chapter 10 is devoted to a space of learning to write a new chapter in your life. The previous chapters gave nourishment and some strength to your tired caregiver nature; this one focuses on the new stories that you can tell. You will begin to count the cost of living with a family member by focusing on the actions and events where you have the power to make positive changes within your home. You are provided a view of what acceptance, forgiveness, and rewriting outdated traditional family roles can look like while LIVING the Good Life.

At the end of each chapter you will be offered one or more concrete actions found in the form of a reflective exercise. These exercises will help you to explore and record your own stories where the caretaker self and the caregiver self can learn to work together. The exercises will build upon each other as you move through this book. Using them you can discover some immediate effects of calming the chaos and exploring a new way to view your own needs while navigating demanding lifestyle changes.

The very last exercise in chapter 10 is one that I have seen used by social workers, ministers, and healthcare workers as a way to introduce self-care. This one will specifically explore how personal healing can be discovered in acceptance. In this final exercise you can begin to see a larger view of the road map within your family history. You will create your own genogram chart and then learn ways to chart your path to more rewarding relationships with adult family members- a whole new world can open up before you.

Seeing a new world of possibilities, guided by our own unique essential caring selves, is a beautiful adventure to begin. I hope this book will offer you needed nourishment and vital strength to allow reflective learning that will happen on this adventure. While you are seeking patterns of healthy and not-so-healthy actions or beliefs, you can also taste the sweetness of the discerning fruit you inherited from family history. Kierkegaard said it best: "Life can only be understood backwards; but it must be lived forwards."

My prayer is for you to find the courage to start telling the simple tale of uncovered beliefs, infused with reflection on what were once hidden steps, leading to the healing balm for our many wounds. Mainly, I hope this book will offer you a view of the past through the eyes of an adult instead of unchallenged childhood memories or culturally driven narratives, then we can all walk forward into lives of rewarding relationships with our families and ourselves.

The following story is my own rewriting of family stories when using a genogram chart and open-ended questions to prompt a retelling. That said, I introduce this story because it is where I heard my midlife call to seminary—and then the beginning of my own journey—into writing this book. Shalom.

Hello,

My name at birth was Mary Elizabeth Bushong. Mary was my paternal grandmother. A dress-wearing, book-loving, legal secretary who was such a good Baptist that when I was an infant she carried me down to her church and had me re-baptized since she did not witness the first one, and she wanted to make sure it "took."

Elizabeth was my maternal great aunt, a Midwestern accounting regulations' writer who spent her free time dancing down at the Arthur Murray studios. She was also the favorite aunt within the family even though it was whispered, "She is one of those feminist-lesbian Presbyterians."

The surname Bushong comes from the French word for "little bushes" and that is where the story of my name could end, but it doesn't. To some people, stories of ancestors and origins are not all that interesting, so they will stop reading now (if they haven't already). To others, what I say next… may smack of heresy. You see, what I believe is that if I had to be born a "little bush," then I would choose to be like that bush in Exodus that would never burn up. That little burning desert bush who allowed a floating-slave-baby-turned-murdering-prince to hear his calling to be a prophet. A little bush, burning because of the loving truths, heard from deep within, by a voice named: The Great I AM.

*So here I am, an author, a practical theologian, a willingly burning bush… weaving a story of captives that have found ways to walk away from bondage and who get filled up on the best-tasting, never-ending fruit all along the way. I will give a voice that declares: theology—and therefore religion—is **not** about rules, or laws, or regulations, but about being made in the image of the Creator, who spoke into existence everything good.*

As the author and perfecter of my own faith, I am claiming that my family reminds me daily that our humanity constantly needs union with our divinity. That we can all choose to stop and look when a fire is burning in our hearts because that is where humanity and divinity are meeting in the most unlikely of places—a burning bush, the cool of the garden, and even within a pregnant unwed Jewish woman named Mary.

Chapter 1

The Essence of
a Caring Person

All real living is meeting.
– **Martin Buber**

*Deciphering our family secrets takes us into the heart of
the family's mysterious power to impact our lives. I call
this journey in the family's secret world soul-searching.
… It asks us to listen to stories without our previous
judgments and our habituated ways of understanding.*
– **John Bradshaw**, *Healing the Shame that Binds*

Life is not a problem to be solved, but a reality to be experienced.
– **Soren Kierkegaard**, Danish philosopher

Karen worked as a dental assistant for 26 years and was sure she could not take the high-pitched sound of the drill for one more minute. The office had been getting on her last nerve since her boss retired and all the changes started. The once small family practice was sold to a group of investors, who built on the name and added more people. It seemed to Karen that all the new owners cared about was making a profit.

Lately, she had been feeling that even the everyday sounds at home were just as hard to ignore, too. Since her adult son moved back home, sometimes she would drive around the neighborhood to delay going in the front door. She knew that when she walked in, the TV would be blaring and yet another big mess—that she had not made—would need cleaning up before she could start cooking dinner. No longer wanting to go to work or be home, she felt she did not have anywhere restful or enjoyable to go anymore.

When I met with Karen to discuss her life in the clan of the sandwich generation, she had come to a tipping point in her work-life balance. Her energy, emotions, and concentration skills were pouring out faster than could be replenished and her life felt out of control.

The term *sandwich generation* applies to people who are living their lives sandwiched between an aging parent and an adult child. In twenty-first century America, there are millions of us and that number is growing faster than we can train professionals to help support this life shift.

I handed Karen a cup of coffee and started our conversation.

"So, Karen," I said. "Could you please get us started by telling me why your adult child lives with you?"

"Well, he doesn't have money for a new place," she said in a desperate tone of voice. He got kicked out of his old apartment for having a dog that was not on the lease."

"Okay, but why does he live with *you*?" I emphasized the word *you* in case she did not hear that my question was about her, not her son.

"Well, his girlfriend's mother is a whack-a-doodle, and she—" Karen crossed her arms and talked louder than before, as though she thought I had not been listening the first time she spoke.

"Um, excuse me, Karen," I softly interrupted. "What I am trying to get clarity on is why your twenty-nine-year-old son *lives ... with ... you?*"

"I told you. He has nowhere else to go," Karen stated sharply. Her anger started to show around the edges of her eyes.

"Really?" I asked. "Nowhere? Your house is the *only* one?"

This is when she gave me that look. You know the look. Like a second head had begun to pop out right between my shoulders, and she couldn't understand why someone so odd was sitting before her.

"Okay, let me ask you this," I began again in an even softer voice. "What if you were not here? Let's imagine, for whatever reason, an illness, an accident, or something has taken *you* out of the equation. Where would your son be living today if your home was not an option?"

Karen's face twisted like she had licked a lemon, and she replied, "I don't want to think about those things. I am here. I can't imagine if my child had nowhere to live. I want him to live with me."

"So, *you want your son to live with you*," I repeated. She had finally said out loud the real reason her son was living with her.

Karen had just experienced a lot of emotions in a very short time span. She went from being confused, to frustrated, to angry, to sad and slightly tearful all within a few minutes because I asked her *one* question about living with her adult child.

That was when I asked her the first of two questions I ask everyone who lives with an aging parent or adult child. It is the question I have started (or ended) my own days with for the last ten years.

"Karen, can you please tell me *what the best thing is* about living with your adult child?"

It took a minute before she spoke, but a slight smile came on her lips and she started to tell me about the time he...

And that was when it happened, that moment.

A slight smile, an unexpected spark, changed the energy in the room. It spread to her eyes, and then back to her mouth in light laughter. Karen experienced that "moment" I love to witness *when people are willing* to (re)tell their story from the point of view of the "best thing about (the other person)." These stories come from a special place. That place is what theologians call the soul or essence; scholars call it presence or self; and gurus call it consciousness or self-awareness. I call it *LIVING* in the good. *LIVING* in the good is where we are seeking and experiencing the many connections between what is both human and divine within us. These connections are precious to our essential selves and throughout this book we will explore open-ended questions like the one Karen used to bring together or unite the spiritual with the human side of our caregiver selves.

The Differences Between the Caretaker Self and the Caregiver Self

As a pastoral caregiver, I see *LIVING* as that space where humanity and divinity get a chance to meet. It is that feeling of calm, when we experience a peace that transcends all understanding. That transcendent moment when we know there is something bigger than ourselves, that connection that brings a sense of well-being. Karen's "best thing about" moment helped her calm her emotions and tap into the powerful source of peace inside her instead of remaining caught in the draining drama of being a constant caretaker and rarely a caregiver.

Caretakers are the busy working people who keep our world functioning. Loosely defined, they are those who support a person, an animal, or someone's property, with physical and emotional general upkeep. Often they are employed to take care of something or someone and are paid accordingly.

Caretakers can work long or short hours, depending on the specific needs of whom or what they are caring for, and those needs will constantly be changing with the seasons of the year. Studies are showing that the average person caring for aging parents will be working up to an additional (read: unpaid) 20 to 40 hours a week within the tasks of providing meals, basic domestic and general hygiene, doctors visits, dispensing medication, finding financial and medical resources, and companionship.

Being our caretaker self is essential to the needs of many in our community. It is our task-keeping, left-brain-thinking, organizational-skill-loving part of ourselves. The caretaker self, for whatever reason, wants to stay busy. It needs to stay busy. Yet, it's also the side of ourselves that craves vacations, or time off, because we know we were also created with a promise we often forget to claim, the promise of a day of rest. "And on the seventh day God rested" (Gen. 2:1–3). Yep, I said it out-loud -even God- rested so why don't we?

Caretakers and Caregivers are different sides of the same person. The Caregiver Self is the essence of our spiritual self. The caregiver is the soulful side of ourselves that challenges the concepts that we are fixed and unchanging beings but are instead beings who are created for the "AHA!" moments in life. The caregiver side knows the impact that care and compassion have on our own hearts and minds *while* we are serving our family. It is that divine part of ourselves that can help us identify our strengths, forgive our weaknesses, and then cultivate both into life-giving successes. It is that sweet spark within us that notices a beautiful sunset, that space between hungry and satisfied, and that whisper which proclaims today was a good day, right before we fall asleep at night.

What if that peaceful, joyful, connected state Karen found in her "best thing about" story is who we really are made to be as caring people? As a former hospital chaplain, I have often witnessed these memorable moments when people meet peace just when they have reached a tipping point. The human and the divine meet in their lives, or, better said, the caretaker and the caregiver meet in their lives. These moments are in the first breath of your newborn child and will be in the last breath of your aging parent. Some of us have felt these moments at weddings, when we watch a bride and groom unite, when we move backward into the memories of our own union while being fully present in the current one.

Simply using a positive story to reframe her reactions to her son, Karen, however briefly, felt hope and joy. She had a moment when she again loved being her son's mother, instead of being the woman who "felt overworked and under-appreciated." It was a LIVING moment when her soul/spirit helped her seek what was good in her life. It was a moment when the divine image she was created to be could remind her of how "very good" she is and how good life could be—as it has been since the beginning of time. It can also be when we are powerfully reminded that we were made in the image of the unconditionally Loving Creator of the universe (Gen. 1:27–31, 2:4–7).

Doing No Harm Does *NOT* Mean Do Nothing

When we want to have more hope or joy while in difficult living situations, our essential caring selves may need help to reframe our actions to allow those moments. I am not talking about living in a Pollyanna moment, where we refuse to *see* what is happening all around us or just go numb to what is hard (or painful) as a way of coping with trauma.

No. No. No.

LIVING in the good requires us to look directly into the areas of our lives that need attention to regain a healthy spiritual and physical life. We are more like surgeons than happy-go-lucky Pollyanna's. How?

Like a surgeon or a doctor, we must pledge to do no harm when we see ourselves in an unhealthy state of living, *but that does not mean* we do nothing. We must notice where the problem is, be observant of where to cut into the flesh, then assess and discern the next steps in healing. We would never want a surgeon to say, "Oh, look, we found a small unidentified mass that is blocking a connection between your heart and your brain. Let's just live with it, shall we?" Umm…No. We would rather have our brains and our hearts working together for optimal health and this is true for our human and spiritual health as well. What if that peaceful, joyful, loving connected state is who we really are made to be—but because we do not consciously connect the spiritual with the physical we lose sight of why we are caregivers at all?

Even a professional caregiver like me had to learn that these meetings of peace can be experienced every day. They do not require a unique or even a large event, like a birth, a death, or a wedding, to arise. I started seeking those moments not just for the feeling but to manifest qualities like open-hearted compassion and the wisdom found in reflection, to hear the spiritual self-soul-spirit, and to start *LIVING* a joyful life, even in difficult times.

But, if these meetings of the body and soul happen all the time, why don't we see them all the time? Hold on to your seats, I suggest this lack of connection more often than not, is because we are caring people.

Wait, what? That sounds wrong. Why would being a caring person *prevent* me from living good moments more often? My favorite spiritual teacher, Parker J. Palmer, would say it is because "the soul is shy and needs to feel safe to come out." Simply put- I had to learn that my caregiver self (my spiritual life) was just waiting to come out and interact with my caretaker self (physical life). I needed to learn how to allow safe spaces for my busy and necessary caretaker self to interact with my peaceful nurturing caregiver self. I needed to come to it slowly (speaking gently with questions) and with unwrapped gifts of spiritual fruit, grown ripe with contemplation, to create daily safe spaces for my humanity to enjoy meeting with my spirituality.

Learning to Use Both Sides of our Essential Caring Self, at the Same Time

As a pastoral caregiver, I base my counseling on the premise that we have both a human and a spiritual side and that they need to operate *together* for us to flourish in our essential selves. To operate together they must meet. By taking care of my own aging parent and adult children, I came to realize that I get so busy doing the wrong things—for what I believed were the right reasons—that I forgot we do not have "to do" things to be a loving person. This realization is at once a source of freedom and shame. It is a vision of what unconditional love can look like and sadly, it can be a form of love we have rarely ever seen before.

Being unconditionally loving, or feeling like we do not have to be/act perfect to be loved, can be an upsetting experience. Many of our societal assumptions and unquestioned solutions lose meaning and can no longer function in a space of being unconditionally loved. Being willing to listen to the essential truths spoken by our essential selves when they are connected together is what Fr. Thomas Merton would have called letting go of our "false self" and what Parker Palmer would call "a hidden wholeness." I have been privileged to have spoken with many students of these spiritual teachers, who say seeking to discover our hidden wholeness or facing our false self is life changing. I suggest, that by allowing ourselves to learn to use both sides of our Essential Caring Selves at the same time was and is life giving for me and the others you will be reading narratives from within this book.

We will talk about this more in the coming chapters, but that leads me to ask: Why would people want their human and spiritual selves to meet more often? Maybe, like me, you have noticed that always doing the right thing—but for unexplored reasons—is making you tired, sick, angry, and somehow a bit bitter and are not really sure why. I will be giving you personal narratives and stories like Karen's in this book, for you to explore how becoming "good" storytellers to our spiritual caregiving selves can coax a better way to live with hard and normal life events. Learning to be conscious of interactions with our human caretaker self and spiritual caregiver self allows us to answer questions which ask: Do I have the freedom and/or confidence to make choices for the good of everyone including myself?

The combined wisdom of our caretaking and caregiving selves can build community stories that liberate our minds and actions from the existing structures (habits, fears, dogmatic roles) that often leave us tired, angry, scared, or shut down when we are in the middle of stressful life situations. We can begin finding answers to how we can take care of our families and ourselves for both spiritual and physical reasons. We can firmly challenge why we want to continue trying to "do it all" and find ways to stop experiencing the anger, frustration, and exhaustion that result from trying to get *it all done*.

We Were Created Physically and Spiritually To *BE* in Communities

Our very DNA is built on us being caregivers in a community. Anthropologists have found evidence that, for thousands of years, whole communities of our nomadic ancestors carried their wounded, crippled, and young from place to place when seeking food and other resources for survival. Why did they do that? The people they were carrying could not contribute to the group's well-being and yet the community expended precious energy transporting them with each move.

This seems counterproductive to survival, right? It's all about survival of the fittest, isn't it? Nope. When re-reading Charles Darwin, we can see that his theory of survival *is not* about being the biggest and the strongest, as commonly believed. It is about being the one who discovers the ability to adapt or change within the sometimes unbearable pressures of an ever-changing world.

Countless studies and curated experiences tell us that humans have an essential need for community and that it is *just as necessary* for our survival as food, water, and shelter from the elements.

Spiritually speaking, we were also created in a community of "others." In the creation story even God was not alone. There were "others" in the discussion during creation of the heavens and the earth (Gen. 1:26). Adam was not complete without Eve because it was not good to be alone (Gen. 2:18). And the only command that Jesus spoke was to "love one another as I have loved you" forcing us into relationships in which to practice our spiritual truths (John 13:34). The biblical concept of caring for "one another" is a main theme in all of Judeo-Christian theology spreading from the Torah all the way into Revelations.

If we were created both physically and spiritually to be in a community, then can we be guided to notice, observe, and assess the need we have for a mind-body-spirit recovery? I believe we can, when we are willing to be guided by questions. Open-ended questions can bring a "slanted way," as Emily Dickinson might say, to create safe spaces in which to tell *all of the truths* found waiting in our shy souls as they are interacting with our human selves. I am going to suggest what may run counter to the deep-listening traditions of the desert fathers and mothers: we do not have to go away (on a spiritual quest) to discover a positive change and a connection to our essential selves.

We need interactions with others to find our own paths into greater spiritual truths. By taking care of our aging parents and adult children, we can experience our humanity-meets-divinity moments right now, right at home.

Exercises

Perhaps you are feeling too overwhelmed taking care of your aging parent or adult children to think of doing one more thing (besides reading this book, of course). These exercises are not one more thing "to do" for others. These exercises are for self care. These exercises are for you; so you may do them in whatever form that feels best for you. There will not be a wrong way or a right way to do these.

I pray as you proceed with this book you will grasp that being willing to do radical self-care is full of choices. For instance, you can choose to do the following exercises in several ways. Some people may take as few as five minutes to answer a question and move on to the next one; others may take a whole hour to answer even one question. You can choose to answer as many or as few as you want.

If you choose to skip the exercises all together that is fine. Just keep reading. I suggest, however, that you stop for a minute before you skip on and begin reading the next chapter to make a promise to your tired, shy soul that you will come back to the exercises when you have finished reading the book. These exercises are where you can find the self care that comes from creating safe spaces to invite both your caretaker self and caregiver self to meet and enjoy time together.

In our first set of exercises you will begin to practice a form of self-care by noticing your own moments of peace.

Preparing to Begin

Get a notebook or folder where you can collect all of your responses and reflections from the exercises together in one space. You may want to review this collection when you need encouragement on the journey of transforming relationships. If you want to have worksheets to guide you please visit my website at www.livingwithmomma.com and download any you may need for free.

Exercises

1. What is the best thing about living with your aging parent? What is the best thing about living with your adult child? If you have more than one parent or child in the home, provide a separate answer for each.

2. Which child or parent was the easiest to answer this question about? Which was the hardest? Be prayerful (in whatever form is most comfortable for you) about the hardest and easiest answers. We will seek understanding to your answers in the next chapter(s).

3. Write out Genesis 1:26–27 and Genesis 2:15–25. Why do you think there are two versions of the creation story? Which one have you heard most often? Which one do you connect with the most and why?

Chapter 2

Finding Meaning in the Experience of Caregiving

There are years that ask questions and years that answer.
– **Zora Neale Hurston**, *Their Eyes Were Watching God*

Love is our true destiny. We do not find the meaning of life by ourselves alone—we find it with another.
– **Thomas Merton**, Catalan Trappist Monk

Twenty years from now you will be more disappointed by the things that you didn't do than by the ones you did do. So throw off the bowlines. Sail away from the safe harbor. Catch the trade winds in your sails. Explore. Dream. Discover.
– **H. Jackson Brown**, American Inspirational Author

In the last chapter, I offered you the question I try to ask myself every day: "What is the best thing about living with your aging parent or adult child?" The second question I offer to you now: "What is one thing you wish you had knew **before** living with your aging parent or adult child?" In this chapter, I tell you how I came upon these two important questions, which I now ask anyone who wants to discuss multi-generational living with me. The following story is how I discovered a curiosity, and a sense of wonder, about becoming a good person instead of unconsciously believing I held the whole truth.

It was a beautiful fall day. I was driving in the Blue Ridge Mountains, where every tree for miles around was showing off in that rare explosion of color that occurs for only a few weeks a year. I was on my third cup of coffee but still felt tired, so I pulled into a McDonald's drive-thru to get a cold sweet tea (equal parts caffeine and sugar right there, baby). Suddenly, I woke to the sound of a car honking. Loudly. Behind me. I had fallen asleep in the drive-thru lane. I directed the anger surging through my body into my eyes, which I focused into the rearview mirror in one of those "if looks could kill" moments. I mean, really. My mother was dying after a twelve-year battle with cancer. I still had three hundred miles left to drive. That dude could just take a chill pill.

Then adrenaline kicked in. I started shaking. I had gone from being asleep, to being scared, to angry, to horrifically ashamed when I realized I had fallen asleep at the wheel in a McDonald's drive-thru. The few working brain cells I had left started screaming: "Whoa! I'm so glad the honk came from behind me. What if I fell asleep going seventy-five miles per hour? I could have killed someone. Just rest a few minutes, girl. Pull. Over. Now. And rest." Thankfully—unlike that morning, when I got in the car too tired to drive—I finally listened to my inner self telling me what I needed. I drove directly over to the lone tree in the McDonald's lot, parked, opened the sunroof, turned the volume down on my cell phone, laid back my seat, and feel asleep for two hours.

Finding a Better Way

Caring for people can be extremely stressful. It's a hard job, whether you're a professionally trained caregiver or providing care for a loved one while working another job. But, as discussed earlier, moments of humanity meeting divinity find us, often in unexpected places. This one came to me in a drive-thru. After waking from the best nap I have ever had, three thoughts came to mind on the drive home. "I am alive. No one was hurt. I must find a better way to be a caregiver to myself and my family… at the same time." That was when peace started to calm me to my innermost spaces. I now had a purpose: I became a seeker of ways to have rewarding relationships with my family instead of living like I was the only person available to fulfill unending obligations.

My husband and I became part of the sandwich generation clan around 2007. I did not notice it until, like so many, I hit my tipping point. We were both working, helping an ill parent, and watching our three children fledge from the nest and then boomerang home because of financial and emotional needs. To say these things were straining our marriage would be as much of an understatement as saying I just needed a few minutes to drink a cold tea from McDonald's before I got back on that highway. The family pressures were affecting us financially, emotionally, physically, and spiritually. We were trapped in the middle of "doing good" and saying yes to the next "need" before we even thought to stop and weigh any long-term consequences. We could not see any other choices "since this is just what family does" so we just kept saying yes, while becoming resentful about each one. We were wrong.

When I got home from the drive, where I heard my call to find out how to be a better caregiver to my family and myself, the researcher in me immediately started looking for resources. I found some well-written books giving financial advice and self-care suggestions. Most were professional caregivers' handbooks detailing how to make compassionate decisions *for* aging parents. But as a spiritual seeker, I was conscious of the fact that I also needed help for my own spiritual self so I would stop making decisions *for* my family by hiding it under the guise of being helpful or caring. The problem was, I could not find any written spiritual references that spoke directly to being sandwiched between an aging parent and adult children. I wanted a guide to help me along the path through this complicated life event.

The Clan of the Sandwich Generation

Not finding many written resources, I sought out people to help me and I began to call them my "sandwich clan." They were amazingly real people who were willing to admit to having days when they were on the edge of a good ol' Southern "come-a-part." Some were brave enough to admit that they didn't know whether they could do it all anymore. Together, we created safe spaces to tell each other our personal and sometimes shameful truths that needed to come out of hiding (read: I love my family, but there are days when I do *not* want to live with them).

Many people in this special clan had been developing the skills of compassionate listening. Yeah! I say. I did not want any more advice. I needed people who would listen compassionately and who could tell their own stories for me to learn from. Patterns began to emerge; some people were able to create a culture of self-examination, open communication, and teamwork within their households, sadly others were not. What was the difference between the two outcomes?

'There are years that ask questions and years that answer'

When talking to people about living in multi-generational homes, I have found there are two dominant patterns.

The first pattern is of caring people who know that they need to be constantly learning how to develop abilities and emotional skills in order to be connected to people in healthy ways. Their main beliefs are based around knowing they cannot control a relationship; they can only control their half of a relationship. One such person, whom I have come to admire from our discussions, told me the following story:

"I did not have a very happy childhood. My mother abandoned me into the care of my grandmother. When we were together she was never a really warm person. I did not want to be one of those clingy people that did everything they could think of to make their mother love them. Recently, I discovered that while I may have stopped myself from begging her for attention, I had not protected my heart from growing bitter about it all. I am now learning, each day, how to become better and not bitter."

The second of the two patterns is of caring people who need almost constant validation to prove they are doing good work. They believe that caring, like being loving, is something they already know how to do. Learning how to be a caring person challenges their core identity. They believe if they have to work at having good, long-lasting relationships then something is fundamentally wrong with them or fundamentally wrong with the other person. Often tragically, they think people should **just know how** to treat each other. One such person told me the following story:

"I don't get today's kids at all. They are so lazy, They don't work. They sit at the dinner table and look at their phones the whole meal. In my day, if I ignored my mother like they do she would have made sure I never had a phone again. I told my daughter she should stop her children from always being on their phones, but she never listens to me."

Both of the stories above come from caring, loving people. Both people are sharing homes with adult family members while working full-time jobs. The difference is the first one believes learning is exciting and does not threaten her self-image. The second one has a hard time because she wants to control other people's behaviors and finds it challenging when she cannot persuade them to live her way. To the first person, caring is about connecting to people; to the second person, caring is about proving she is good by being right.

What if I told you that the above two stories were told by the same person? Is it possible that someone could be so was insightful about her past relationships but still be closed-minded about present relationships? Since I already told you I had come to admire her, you would be safe to assume that this lady, named Myra, went on to learn how her uncomfortable assumptions were driving a wedge between her and her daughter. The good news is that Myra chose to become a 78-year-old learner of new social skills, began seeking valuable virtues, and accepting the fruitful gifts that were being offered to her.

She began to accept the unexplored experiences of others (e.g. the important and useful skills of cell phones to a younger generation) as real and valid. She began by learning to speak with her daughter and her grandchildren within the goal of understanding different perspectives. She grew confident that instead of making assumptions in an effort to prove loved ones wrong, she had to learn how to ask herself and others questions that were open ended and non-threatening. (eg. How do I use email and text messages to better understand my grandchildren?) Myra no longer held the useless and discrediting idea that she held *the only* truth in the room. She refused the old adage and proved that it is possible to teach "old dogs new tricks."

'We do not find the meaning of life by ourselves alone—we find it with another.'

Some of the people in my sandwich clan hold firmly to outdated beliefs and refuse to open their hearts to learning new ways to connect. They are still singing the same bluesy song of "constant sorrow" when they talk about living with their families. I don't talk with them often, but if I run into them when we are both shopping at the Piggly Wiggly, then I have to ask the polite "how are you doing" question. (Honestly, there are one or two people, if I see them—before they see me—that I am sorely tempted to run and duck into another aisle. But my momma taught me better than that.)

These are the people that are stuck in the loop of debate about how their "family" is never going to change. We have all been there in one form or another. For whatever reason, we stop caring about making a connection with someone and insist on proving we are right by discrediting their views. We listen only deep enough to find the "flaws" in what they are saying as a way to protect ourselves. Sometimes we may even fall further into opposition mode and refuse to find meaning in what others think or feel because of a condition that social scientists call "othering."

"Othering" is a process where a conscious or unconscious assumption is made to identify a group or an individual as being different than "the self." It is not a new concept. It has been experienced since the beginning of time. Educators tell us we learn languages by comparing terms to each other (e.g., hot vs. cold, up vs. down). So, simply put, social "othering" is putting labels (they are vs. we are) to show differences between people. That's not a bad thing (e.g., I have red hair vs. Karen has blonde hair) unless it also means "we" are right and therefore "they" are wrong (e.g. They are all bad, lazy, dumb, evil, etc.).

People who cannot learn new ways to connect while being in a community comprised of close family interactions seem to get stuck in feeling alone and sorrowful. They are held captive to outdated beliefs that tell them there is only one way to think or only one way that is right. Many of these people also believe "the truth shall make you free," yet I suggest that this narrows the meaning of this sacred text. It has been totally taken out of context of when, to whom, and maybe even why this was said in the Book of John (John 8: 31-32).

Then there are those who want to bravely explore new ways to care and communicate in order to connect. They have nothing to prove but merely want to connect with people. They have discovered how to find a deeper meaning from being in a vibrant community and they want others to enjoy this with them. They display characteristics that bring others to ask them "How are you, honey?" and mean it. These are the people who are finding their own moments when the caregiver and caretaker selves are working together.

These are the people who are filled with the new opportunities they have found by seeking "love, peace, joy, patience, kindness, goodness, gentleness, and self-control … in ever-increasing measure." They say things like: "*I am becoming excited about all I am learning. I am not feeling as angry or exhausted anymore. I thought I was a patient person, but now I see where I can grow in that area of my life.*" Trust me, it's like a big drink of cool water when a pastoral caregiver does not need to be with or comfort a person anymore *because* they are doing well on their own. Where do we find these opportunities to be filled up with the amazingly refreshing virtues, character traits, and fruitful lives?

Virtues, Character Traits and the Fruit of the Spirit

Author William Bennett called these divinely refreshing abilities *virtues*. Thomas Jefferson called them *character traits* and spent his whole life working to develop them in his character. Aristotle called them means of *excellence*. It was the apostle Paul who called them fruits of the Spirit, and the pastoral caregiver in me knows this is where the human and divine moments can come together. I have seen what can happen when good people are in difficult situations, which is where practical theology flourishes. Practical theology is not just knowing a scripture; it is applying practical solutions in response to AHA! moments which can allow us to be fully alive *inside* scripture. Remembering and holding tightly with actions to ripen the the promise of fruitful living in Galatians is where the human and the divine can meet on a regular basis. Paul claims we already have been gifted with fruit of the Spirit (Gal. 5:22/3) "The fruit of the Spirit is love, joy, peace, patience, kindness, goodness, gentleness and self-control" AND "in ever-increasing measure." Those gifts just keep on coming.

As I mentioned in Chapter 1, I was seeking a way for both my caretaker self and my caregiver self to work together. My caregiver self could find rest and safe spaces in the promises of Wisdom (another word for Spirit) and receiving what is Holy. Practically speaking, with that promised fruit, I am able to step out of those fixed mindsets of what being a good person looks like and begin to embrace spiritual growth alongside any of my human actions. That said, what can LIVING be if we learn to look through a lens of our divine gifts while choosing to consciously interact with our both of our essential caring selves? It looks like a good life. When we choose to be consciously LIVING with the divine gifts creates a safe place to identify strengths, forgive weaknesses, and cultivate useful traits or habits for both of our physical and spiritual selves in everyday life.

Claiming that the Spiritual and Physical Selves Can Interact

So how do we experience those caregiver moments where we are given divine fruit without it being all "woo-woo" weird or wishy-washy-fairy-tale make believe, or even just some plain old hopeful thinking? How do we even attempt to claim that the spiritual and the physical can interact at all? The author of Hebrews claims ancient texts are "living and active" (Heb. 4:4). More to the point, if I can look at scripture from the view of being alive with me, then I can see it as a safe space from which to reflect my own story in/with/beside a loving Creator. This allows me to reshape, replace, or remove negative or unfruitful reactions in my life, right now and in the future. I cannot fail, just grow—nice, huh? Practical theology, like love, is a gerund—it can be both a noun and a verb and actually must be to allow its full meaning to be displayed.

Yeah right, now what do you do… if it is a spiritual thing?

Living without regrets has been a theme within my family. That is probably why I love the quote from the author H. Jackson Brown, which is placed at the beginning of this chapter. It summarizes what seeking meaning as a caregiver is all about. Brown wrote *Life's Little Instruction Book* as a going-away present to his college-bound son. "Twenty years from now you will be more disappointed by the things that you didn't do than by the ones you did do. So throw off the bowlines. Sail away from the safe harbor. Catch the trade winds in your sails. Explore. Dream. Discover."

Exploring, dreaming and discovering is something I love to do with my caregiving self and that is what I pray this book is going to show you how to do, too. Seeking how my caregiver self is being fed fruits "*with ever-increasing measure*" means that this is not a one-time thing— these are divine gifts that are unending, unlimited, unregulated, and unmeasurable. Within each chapter, I give narratives from people who are actively seeking and intentionally acting within the fruits they have been given.

I will also more fully define what these spiritual fruits look like so we know what to expect when we accept them and become excited enough to take a big ol' bite out of them. One way to understand each fruit or virtue is to define them using historical and contextual etymology (or origins and original meanings) to help us understand its "true sense" or meanings that have changed over time within translations and cultures. Considering the true sense of a word gives us a more abundant view of the truths in the promises made to us by our Loving Creator. When we look at the meaning of or definition of each fruit. For example, let's start with the the historical and contextual definitions for the word "soul" and see how it also means our spirit and our caregiver self.

Reflecting on Our Soul, Spirit, and Caregiver Self

The word *soul* (*nepes*) occurs more than 780 times in the Hebrew Bible. The basic meaning of the word is essence of life, the act of breathing, or taking a breath. In Genesis (1:20), the phrase "living soul" is used. The King James Version Bible uses twenty-eight different terms for this one Hebrew word, including *soul*, *self*, and *life*.

So what is the difference between soul and spirit? Why are they are so tightly woven together that they can be interchangeable when translating texts from one language to another? They are different, right? Yes. The word *spirit* has nine different meanings, but for the sake of this chapter on caregiving spirit, I am going to concentrate on its meaning as breath (*ruah*).

When we are in spaces of reflection, our ruah/soul is described as a gentle, refreshing evening breeze. Scripture and ancient texts tell us our spirit is not only a breath but that it has its own agency it can also see, hear, smell, touch and taste when spoken as an analogy within our relationship and community with the Creator. Our soul, ruah, was with/in the first humans in the Garden of Eden, and it is with us even when we forget to be in spaces to reflect on our spiritual experiences. In Genesis 3:8, it reads: "... they heard **the voice of the Lord God** *walking in the garden in the cool of the day.*" I mean, really, how does someone hear a voice walking? That is stunningly rich sensory language, found in the translations of scriptures from Hebrew to English.

If that doesn't make your senses tingle a bit, consider that *ruah* can also mean a mindset or a disposition, as when David says, "Uphold me with thy free Spirit," referring to his inner disposition or emotions. When used in 1 Peter, it also means heart, soul, mind, spirit, and life. This is our essential caregiver self wanting to actively bring our mind-body-spirit into a perfect union which is humanity meeting divinity within us.

When we look at our caregiver self—or our spirit—with this broader view it also can be the very core of our personality, which can also become the behaviors that are acted out by our caring selves. What I am suggesting here, is a seamless connection between our caretaker self and our caregiver self. As I have mentioned before, the spirit that an unconditionally loving Universal Creator breathed into us must be paid attention to. God breathed life into us. Breathing is essential to life, yet we do not even have to think in order for it to happen.

My sandwich clan taught me to start seeing how Galatians 5:22 can allow me to pay attention to my true self, caring essence, or spirit/soul filled with the gifts of love, joy, peace, patience, kindness, gentleness, goodness and self-control. After we realize this, we now can ask: "*What is the one thing I wish I knew before (living with my aging parent or adult child)?*" and get an answer that can lead us to *LIVING* in the good of our essential selves.

When I asked myself the open-ended question, *What is the one thing I wish I knew before committing to driving home each month to clean my mother's house*, I came up with the following answers: I wish I knew how hard (read: physically exhausting and downright dangerous) it was going to be to drive more than six hundred miles roundtrip (for years). I wish I knew how to stop the actions (no matter how well-intended they may have started out as being) that were bringing me to my tipping point. I wish I knew what actions I could do that allowed me to let her know that I loved her, supported her, and was going to miss her terribly when she was gone.

In the following chapters we will explore some of the paths caregivers are using while being inspired to use practical theology as a safe space, to learn and grow in their essential caring natures. In the next seven chapters we will use the acronym L.I.V.I.N.G. to help us focus on each of the promised gifts of the Holy Spirit or the virtues that so many people across time have been consciously seeking. There are seven simple steps for *LIVING* that I have identified from reading hundreds of books and articles on changing your mindset, identifying your core identity, or seeking spiritual direction which allows you powerful ways to live. I have seen people who focus on these seven steps become powerful learners.

These are people who show the courage to claim their divine gifts as being unending, unlimited, and unregulated in their mind-body-spirit connection.

L—Loving Your Peace. The life-giving actions of embracing a wholeness of our mind, body, and spirit.

I—Integrity of Goodness. The ability to encourage with honesty that avoids all forms of harshness or cruelty by holding others in high esteem.

V—Valuing Patience. Having a high opinion or respecting someone by yielding to the benefits of hope despite their actions.

I—Insightful Self-Control. The ability to discern when our impulses, desires, or emotions should be tempered, by considering that people are made in the image of a Divine Creator.

N—Nonjudgmental Faith. The ability to adjust negative assumptions of others toward a more complete confidence believing people are doing the best they can with what they have been given.

G—Guiding Joy. A measurable wellness or delight found in being thankful for our community and our family.

On this powerful journey we are about to embark on, may we again consider the wisdom of Thomas Merton: "Love is our true destiny. We do not find the meaning of life by ourselves alone—we find it with another."

Suggested Exercise

This exercise will help prepare you for learning to use reflective journaling as a compass in the coming chapters. Reflective journaling is where you can begin to see some of your own AHA! moments of connection between your spiritual and physical self. They are the moments of connection that will come from reflecting on open-ended questions and where you can find *your own* meaningful experiences simply because you are a caring person.

Before you begin: Pick (only) one person you wrote a "best thing about" response (see Chapter 1 exercises). Re-read that response. You are re-reading your response to allow a positive (or lighter) tone to be the frame from which you will explore needs. If you are not feeling close to (e.g., if you feel mad, sad, or hopeless) to this person after reading your "best thing" response, consider the following options:

Re-read it again, but this time out loud.

Re-write the response from a new perspective or write an entirely different "best thing" narrative.

Choose a different person you wrote a story about; this one may not be a safe space for your spirit to start practicing these exercises with.

Next we will begin to explore your gifts and virtues from within the answers you will give in the following exercise. Often an identified need or virtue comes laden with heavy emotions in the beginning. That's okay, you are among friends who are sharing their own AHA! moments in this book. We are all using sacred texts as a safe space for spiritual awakenings. We are all finding a higher meaning to caring than, "It's just what family does."

In the same notebook as before, please answer the following questions:

1. What is the one thing you wish you knew before _____ (name of your aging parent or adult child) moved in with you? Please **only** write one person's name in the space provided. You may find that you are writing more than one thing, that is fine, too. Let it all out. You may need to write it down on paper to make it seem more real. Just make sure you go back and read what you wrote and then narrow it down to one sentence.

2. If you could choose any person in your family (living or not) to have a good meal with who would you choose and why?

3. Write out Galatians 5:22-23. Writing out sacred text can help us slow down our thoughts. This can help you prepare for further reflective journaling which we will begin to practice in the following chapters.

Chapter 3

Loving Your Peace

The secret to change is to focus all of your energy,
not on fighting the old, but on building the new.
— **Socrates**, 4th century philosopher

Blessed are the peacemakers, for they
shall be called children of God.
— **Jesus**, Sermon on the Mount

Everything can be taken from a man but one thing: the
last of the human freedoms—to choose one's attitude in
any given set of circumstances, to choose one's own way.
— **Viktor Frankl**, Man's Search for Meaning

Martha worked in the hospitality industry. At middle age, she had to move into the "family home" to take care of her aging father, who was refusing nursing care or as he called it, help from strangers. Adding to Martha's grief were the unforeseen stressors she experienced sharing the family home with her adult sister and brother. Over the past couple of years, they had all come home as a way to make ends meet or to help with their father's care since the death of their mother.

Martha admitted to having a great relationship with her brother. He was the baby of the family, and even though he had always been a bit distracted, "his heart was in the right place." She also discussed experiencing some contention with her younger sister. Even before this living arrangement, maybe because she was the oldest, Martha often felt her siblings took advantage of her with some unreasonable expectations. She wished she could just "relax and have some fun" like everyone else around her seemed to be doing.

Martha hadn't talked directly to her siblings about how she felt when their friends just showed up at the house, but it made her mad. She did not want to fight but "they know that I work full-time, too." She usually kept quiet and just did what everyone expected from her.

Martha described herself as pretty even tempered. In the past she did not want to "make waves," but she had begun blowing her top, faster and more frequently. She was totally embarrassed by these outbursts, especially this last time. She lost it in front of both family and friends. It all started after a hard day at work when she came home to find a house full of people (including people she said that she loves) just sitting around at dinner time, "like they were waiting to be served or something." Martha decided to give them all a piece of her mind. "It was like, I just can't do this anymore."

That's when Martha stormed straight up to Jesus Christ and said: "Lord, don't you care that my sister has left me to do the work by myself? Tell her to help me!"

And Jesus said, "No" (Luke 10:38–41).

A Biblical Story for Practical Use

Okay, those of us familiar with the story of Martha, Mary, and Lazarus found in the book of Luke know that Jesus didn't *just* say "No" to Martha's passive aggressive request. There is more to that story, but there are only two sentences mentioned in response to that request and we will focus on these later in the chapter. In the above narrative, I simply showed you a twenty-first century version of a first century story seen through the lens of practical theology.

The purpose of shifting from the life stories I have collected over the years to unexpectedly showing you a biblical narrative was to remind us all that family conflict is as old as time. For that matter, family conflict was the very first story after Adam and Eve left the Garden of Eden. Even two people brought up in a place where everything was "very good" still had some big problems surrounding their adult children. One could say their sons, Cain and Abel, suffered from an extreme case of sibling rivalry. That rivalry became so bad that someone died and the family was split emotionally for generations. The 66 sacred books in Protestant scriptures also hold some pretty wild stories of family conflict and they rarely mention any resolution at all.

Maybe being handed spiritual stories with no obvious solutions are a good thing. Why? Maybe because then we can never assume that there is *only* one way to find resolution to conflict in a world like ours. We live in a world which always needs to find a way back to grace. That might explain why most questions thrown at Jesus were just tossed right back into the crowds in the form of another question. Trauma, drama and hard times happen even in the best families. The sacred scriptures remind us that even our ancestors had to deal with parental favoritism, sibling rivalry, and people lying to get what they wanted. So reading them is beneficial to us on many levels.

The wise among us know that bad things will happen to good people, so they do not feel a need to explain or attempt to pass blame on others when conflict and hard things happen in their lives. Wisdom has taught them that the "secret to change is to focus all their energy not on fighting the old but in building the new." This is why the wisdom of Holocaust survivor and philosopher Viktor Frankl rings so true: "Everything can be taken from a man but one thing: the last of the human freedoms—to choose one's attitude in any given set of circumstances, to choose one's own way."

Choosing Your Own Way

In this chapter, we will start to put the pieces together so that you can wisely "choose one's own way," on a path made clear by the promised fruits of the Spirit. This fruit, when reflected in a refreshing practical theology, can affect positive change and calming actions almost immediately in your family life. How? By following some simple steps built on the answers you found in the suggested exercises in Chapters 1 and 2 and soon here in chapter 3, we will begin to be guided into Loving Peace within our homes.

If you have not started your notebook or reflective journal yet, that's okay. You have two choices here: 1. You can learn by observing the paths others share within this book (maybe you need to see how others have nourished their essential caring selves before you are ready to seek out your shy soul), or 2. You can stop here and go back just two chapters and write out your answers to the exercises, in order to begin your own journey now.

Now that you have made that choice, let's begin opening up our view by considering we are not the only ones being affected by the dramatic social and lifestyle changes swirling all around us in twenty-first century families. Our rapidly aging population and rising concerns about the vitality of systems of care for baby boomers are a concern of scholars studying family and social systems of recent years. Because life expectancy has increased, the multi-generational family stumbles into previously unheard-of levels of economic growth and scarcity at the same time. For example, the Pew Research Center has discovered that, for the first time in more than a century, Americans ages eighteen to thirty-four are more likely to be living with a parent or other family member than in any other living situation. This shift is occurring across all economic ranges and includes both males and females. According to the National Institute on Aging, up to 40 percent of grandparents provide some care for the children of their working children.

These social shifts can cause us to have many fearful responses to the ways we all must organize our lives, or choose our own ways, around the many uncontrollable variables in our immediate, local, and even global society. What that could mean is, we get self-focused and we forget we are not the only people on these rocky, challenging, heart changing, life treks. It can be very useful for us to remember that we are ALL in this together even when we don't see the others on our path. John Donne's 400-year-old prose against isolationism speaks a larger truth to our need for community when he said, "No man is an island." This challenges the American concepts of " pull up your bootstraps or I made my own way." Most outdated or unexplored concepts like these are knocked down when faced with the reality it like those we are living with now being our aging population and global economic downturns.

It is good to remember we actually depend on people every day, as we walk through life, even if we don't leave the house. For example, you probably woke up this morning to an alarm clock (or phone app) that was made by people you will never meet. You probably drank coffee grown in Latin America and put on clothes manufactured in

China. Even if you buy only "American-made" products most of us do not even have the skills to sew the clothes we wear, much less weave the material or raise the plants or animals at the root of the whole process. All the things we interacted with during the first few minutes of our day depended on others. That gives us all a very loose but personal connection to other people.

That said, as we learn to live in more fruitful, rewarding family relationships, we will also begin to consider how others in our sandwich generation are shifting, connecting, and affecting our global society. My own scholarly interests in this field are concentrated on the changing structures of multi-generational families and the conflicts that can bond together or break apart a family. Even if you do not live with your aging parent or adult child, just living in proximity to others who do will affect how you spend your time and resources. These are the events that cause dramatic economic and emotional shifts in family dynamics.

I have lived with adult family members, older and younger. This unplanned lifestyle shift forced me to learn how to get my head and heart—and therefore actions—wrapped around a form of practical theology found when reading Martha's passive-aggressive rant in the book of Luke. That basic theology looks like this: Jesus *will not* change the behavior of my family to better serve me. But, wait! I am a good person, right? And as a good person who has many jobs and roles in life (wife, mother, grandmother, pastor, author, friend, sister, daughter, etc.), don't I deserve to have some help from my family? Maybe. But why should I expect my family to change as my only form of help?

On the days I am honest with myself, there were times, just like with Karen and Martha, I would get home and see dirty dishes filling the sink and I would have a hissy fit. I would allow my tired caretaker self to fall into passive-aggressive behaviors—like slamming cabinet doors and loudly unloading the dishwasher *so everyone knew I was doing the dishes, again*. Sometimes my self-pity would simmer for days and then boil over into a good ol' Southern girl "come to Jesus talk" with whomever was at the dinner table that night. In my saner moments, I know that groaning and griping *never* works well as a motivator. But my human caretaker self can still find humor in sentiment embroidered on a dishtowel a friend gave me: "Flogging of all pirates will continue until the crew's morale improves."

When we take a view similar to Martha's, wanting Jesus to fix our families' squabbles, we are translating, interpreting, and applying scripture literally or historically in an unhealthy way. Instead, because we're not limited to seeing through a two-thousand-year-old lens, when we apply practical theology, we can see what is holy in the story, understanding new choices we can make our way toward. These are the spaces where our humanity and divinity can meet to give fruitful options to ourselves and our families.

Choices that are Loving, Peaceful and Caring

Choosing ideas from the lens of practical theology helps me to keep it simple: In my saner moments I know I cannot change anyone other than myself. Simply put, I look at my own life events through the lens of Love and Peace (that's as practical as theology can get). Why love and peace? These are the first two gifts of the Spirit that we already possess. These are the very first fruits we are told we have been given in ever-increasing measure by sacred scriptures. (Eph.5:22)

In the area of my life that resembled Martha's dilemma, could I be brave enough to choose to *acknowledge* where peace was not yet strong in me? Could I do something that helps me become my own caregiver and therefore feed my spirit/soul with needed nourishment that comes from accepting a gift of love or peace? Yes. How? We can choose to become stronger by acknowledging our own forms of Martha's hissy fit. How? We begin to walk toward more healthy, fruitful reactions that bring steady growth to our spirit and heart instead. Let's explore what that can look like for each of us.

I need to be brave enough to acknowledge where my peace needs growth—first, let's say what spiritual growth is *not*. It is *not* feeling guilty. Admitting a weakness is not to be confused with, nor should it feel like, shame. Beating ourselves up or shaming ourselves just gets in the way of learning. That's why shaming or blaming the family at the dinner table during one of my own hissy-fits could not produce a good or lasting effect on the amount of disorder in my home. No one is motivated to make a positive change with negative accusations. We are created in a "very good" place, and we are created in the image of an unconditionally Loving Creator so guilt and shame are a waste of energy that could be better used by enjoying our new life of loving peace.

If you suffer like I do at times from shame, blame, or guilt, then I suggest you choose to learn how to remove these thorns from your flesh. My favorite shame-removal teacher is Brené Brown. She writes beautifully about how our perfectionist, to-do-list-making, conflict-avoiding, people-pleasing culture is eroding our true selves. I have her books listed on the bibliography pages should you want one for yourself.

What acknowledging where our peace needs growth *does* look like: finding the spaces where we want and can act more loving, and peaceful to ourselves and our families. By coming up with real-life ways to turn our everyday actions onto the path where the divine and the human meet our families and become life-giving instead of life-draining. Practicing Love and Peace can clean-out our fear-filled narratives (e.g. I will never be good enough, they will never appreciate me) into more encouraging universal truths (I don't need to save others, I am born in the image of the Creator, I am good enough).

Loving Your Peace, Defined

Definitions of *love* and *peace* have been so thoroughly watered down from overuse that I suggest we consider the original definitions to hear wisdom or get some clarity on these universal truths.

The word *love* is found more than five hundred times in Hebrew and Christian scriptures. *Love* in Hebrew is described by the action of (life) giving. One spiritual definition of love is: "Love is patient, love is kind. It does not envy, it does not boast, it is not proud. It does not dishonor others, it is not self-seeking, it is not easily angered, it keeps no record of wrongs" (1 Cor. 13:4–8). Love exists within actions.

While this definition of love may be larger than I had normally allowed in my life, it is the definition of *peace* that surprised me. *Peace* is usually taken to mean lack of conflict or the stopping of war. The real definition is personal and intimate enough for use on a daily level. The word *peace* is an extremely important term in Hebrew scriptures (*shalom*), where it means a "wholeness of mind and body." It is a form of being complete or unhurt. *Peace* is used more than four hundred times, in scriptures, in the context of being complete, whole, and unharmed. How does this look in a practical sense when it comes to us loving our peace?

Being intentionally aware that *LIVING* with the definition of Loving our Peace is when we are seeking ways for the life-giving actions to embrace our wholeness of our mind, body, and spirit. When we live out scriptural love and peace with our caring selves, we give and are given unconditional wholeness. For example, when Martha stormed into the room with her passive-aggressive demands directed at her family and at Jesus (expecting them to change because of misguided dogmas or culturally taught roles), she was not *being* loving, even though she was *doing* the loving act of making a meal. She was giving food to renew the energy of her family and friends. Yet, I suggest her caretaker self and caregiver self were not in sync with each other at all. Providing a meal for her friends and family was no longer love but a burden, and she made everyone else know that her load was heavy.

When I explain this "Martha was not being loving" idea to people, they often give me the frozen "what are you saying" look. Some immediately fight, saying, "Who is going to make the meal then? They have to eat, right?" Others—and these scare me the most—say, "Okay, I will just *be* more loving then," and they do nothing more than glance in the mirror, forgetting that *being* loving is not about putting on a happy face while continuing to resentfully serve (just more quietly that is) or assuming a misused "attitude of gratitude" as a caretaker. No, loving your peace is about spending time listening to what your loving caregiver self wants to say in this situation.

More than one love story is being written here, and there is more than one way to (re)write it. The first story can acknowledge that Martha is being a caretaker for all the meals and the details of the meals. The anger she feels shows that this is not good for Martha's caregiver soul. She must get brave and ask herself why she is acting angry. How? Use the second question I gave you. "What is the one thing I wish I knew before I agreed to be the meal maker?" She did not know how to ask for what she needed because she could not hear her caregiver-self asking for nourishment over the loud, stressed-out actions her caretaker/ human self just automatically kept doing. How could Martha choose to make the family meals, or not make the family meals? Can both options become a time of renewal and not an obligation? Was she really the only one that had to make all the meals for everyone?

Embracing Life-Giving Stories

What can we then choose as our (re)written story about love and peace in our lives? For me, to bravely look at my own automatic responses took a lot of journaling. I give you the chapter exercises for helping you to start your own spiritual journaling journey. After I had that life-changing nap in the McDonald's drive-through, I wanted to see why the conflict with my caretaker self was happening with my caregiver self. How could Martha's story, in Luke, allow me to look at my story and see if my assumptions (whose job it is to make dinner anyway?) can at times be fodder for outdated roles or stereotypes that keep me from loving, peaceful truths? How was my self-imposed role of being the one to always make dinner or keep the house tidy an outdated role? How is bravely questioning my actions good for anyone?

Let's look at the steps Karen, from Chapter 1, took concerning her feelings, which came at the end of a long work day. To recap: Karen was living with her adult son, who left messes all over her home, which she believed was forcing her to drive around mindlessly instead of just going home after work.

Karen chose to begin living within the definition of Loving our Peace. She began seeking ways for the life-giving actions to embrace her wholeness of her mind, body, and spirit. She reviewed her journal exercises, re-reading her answers to the questions "What is the best thing about…?" and "What do I wish I knew before my son moved in?" She condensed her pages and pages of journaling into one sentence for each question. Then she asked herself, "where are the safe spaces I enjoy and what are the things I do that give me a sense of peace?" For her final response, she had some fun creating a list of actions she could refer to when she needed to give her caregiver self a safe place to enjoy loving her peace. Here is what she wrote:

1. The best thing about living with my son is his ability to make me laugh.
2. The thing I wish I knew before he moved in is how much more time I would spend cleaning up after him (and the consequences of those actions) rather than laughing with him.

3. My favorite things to do that give me a sense of peace: (1) listen to music, (2) soak in a bubble bath, and (3) go for long walks.

Karen now had a plan of intentional actions to help her remember to feed peace to her caring self. It was her own personal guide to loving her peace. The actions she chose could be concisely used to replace the moods of anger, frustration, and self-pity (her words, not mine) with peace and love. Karen began to chose peaceful actions to replace her angry reactions.

The day after creating her guiding list, Karen was prepared before walking into a trashed kitchen. She was choosing not to react with anger but with the fruit of love and peace that she already had been given in ever-increasing measure. This is what she did instead: She walked in her house. She saw the mess and chose to use her plan. She put on her earphones to listen to music which she had preloaded for such a time as this. She put the dirty dishes in soapy water, and spent some time mindfully enjoying the bubbles. Then she cooked dinner in a state of peace.

I hope you have noticed I have not said *anything* (yet) about her son's behavior. Nothing had changed in that area. What I am saying is that by concentrating on what *she* could change, Karen allowed her spirit to feed on the fruit of love and peace for her caregiver spirit. Slowly things began to change in her outer world as her divine and human selves met-up in those moments formerly wasted on hissy fits and self-pity.

Just Be Real, Not Perfect

What happened that first night Karen decided to love her peace? Did a miracle occur? Did her son fall to his knees and say, "Oh, dear mother, I see all that you do for me and the entire world. Let me have that soapy sponge and forgive me for all the ways I do not appreciate you"?

Nope. No way. Her son did absolutely nothing. Nada. Zip. Remember she did not do this to make him change, but to feed her essential caring spirit.

But that does not mean that nothing happened. Karen chose not to spend all her energy slamming cabinet doors and passive-aggressively making sure everyone feared her wrath. She actually felt better that evening. And she kept at it.

The next night, she did the same actions as she did on the first. The kitchen was becoming a space of peace and not chaos for her. There was no nagging, complaining, or mentioning how hard she works to anyone within earshot. Her caregiving soul (as well as her son's) was beginning to feel safe enough to come out. Karen kept journaling and exploring what love and peace meant to her. Some nights, when she came home, she just *could not do the housework* without being angry. That was okay. She was not trying to be perfect, only more peaceful and loving.

Those nights when she could not move past her anger, she would choose to use the third activity she had put on her list of things that bring her peaceful feelings: Karen would go for a walk. She admitted to me that her daily step count was higher than it had ever been, but eventually things began to change. Karen was able to notice when she had been treating her son like a child and as a result why he may have kept living childishly around her. She then became aware she was ready to start a discussion with her son about what she needed. Adult to adult. It was a full-circle moment when she saw she needed to respect her son like the 29-year-old man he was. That AHA! moment allowed her to talk with respect—not command, not demand, not demeaningly, but lovingly talk—about what she would like help with around the house that they were both living in.

Karen and her son sat down together and organized a chore chart. Then she began treating him like an adult roommate in many other ways, too. But first she had to start by loving her peace to make room for the good ideas growing in her well-fed mind/heart/and spirit. One idea that came to her was when she noticed that if she unloaded the dishwasher every morning, while the coffee was brewing, the number of dishes left in the sink that day was drastically reduced. The empty dishwasher was a now a convenient place to set them, for both her and her son.

She also noticed that when she kept to her budget by cooking instead of defaulting to fast food and her increased walking was helping her to be able to meet her health goals. She felt happier, more confident, which helped her relationships outside of the home improve too. Then even bigger things happened. One evening when she was making dinner, her son came into the kitchen and *actually talked* with her. They laughed. They listened. They grew. Meanwhile, each day Karen was growing stronger in her spiritual gifts of peace and love. Each day she made choices to act more loving and peaceful no matter what those around her chose to do. Her spiritual gifts of peace and love were growing in ever-increasing measure.

Suggested Exercises

If you have chosen to do these exercises to bring peace, love and goodness into your caregiver spirit then please begin the following exercises.

1. Pick one person in your home about whom you have written a "best thing about" story and summarize that statement in one sentence. Does that sentence make you smile and feel good inside, or does it bring up tension? How does your body react to this sentence? Are your shoulders tensed up around your neck? Do you feel sad?
2. If you are feeling negative emotions, check your sentence and make sure you have summed up what you enjoy about the person and not something you are angry about.

3. Consider your answer to the second question, "What is the one thing you wish you knew before your aging parent or adult child moved in with you?" Write in one sentence what you need to see change. It looks like this:

4. I need to _____ more with _____ instead of _____ for _____.

5. (For example, Karen could write: "I need to laugh more with Joe instead of being so angry at him for making messes around the house.")

6. Pick three (or more) key activities you can *do* that give you a sense of peace. Don't sabotage this list with answers like "go to Hawaii" and "lay on the beach" unless you have a way of making those into real actions that you can do immediately or every day.

7. Rewrite a story for your caregiving self that includes one new way of living with an aging parent or an adult child in the above sentence. Ask yourself where you feel the lack of divine and human connection in your caregiver self and make a plan for loving your peace the next time you are faced with anger or sadness instead of peace.

8. Write out the actions of love given in 1 Cor. Love is patient and kind, neither envious or boastful, not proud, self-seeking, nor easily angered. How can these actions speak to you Loving your Peace. How can being patient add to your wholeness of body and mind, or a the sense of being complete and unharmed?

9. Write out the definition we hold for Loving our Peace. *Peace is the wholeness of body and mind, the sense of being complete and unharmed.* Pick one thing you can you do in concrete terms within your own "I wish I knew" stories for peace to be around your spirit? If *Blessed are the Peacemakers*, then what does being called *a child of the Creator* mean in your life?

10. Consider writing yourself a pledge to be more conscious of life-giving vs. life-draining actions. An example you can use: "I will be more conscious of my life-giving actions as a way to apply a healing salve to my wounded and tired spirit. I will not dishonor others by _____ (use a passive aggressive action you see that you fall into) any longer. I will live as though I am the only person I can change, as a way to be patient with loved ones and for safe spaces to allow growth to occur with my caretaker and caregiver selves."

Please note all of the suggested exercises are not intended to help people in abusive relationships. These exercises are not meant to allow or enable behaviors associated with abusive people in any way shape or form. Period. No one was holding abusive power over Martha, Karen, or me in the previous scenarios. If you are in an abusive situation, with a spouse or an adult child, please seek immediate help from a trained professional. Also consider using the resources found at the end of this book if you are trapped in the whirlwind of a relationship fueled by alcohol, drugs, physical, or mental abuse.

Chapter 4

Integrity of Goodness

"How you love anything is how you love everything. Love is a quality of relationship more than a statement about the worthiness or deservedness of the object loved."
– **Richard Rohr**, author and Franciscan Friar

"Be kind whenever possible. It is always possible."
– **Dalai Lama, 14th**

"The best of our stories are those that transform and redeem us, ones that both ground us in ourselves by reminding us what it means to be human and elevate us by furnishing an instrument of self-transcendence."
– **Neil Gaiman**, English author

Diane was blessed with the strawberry-blonde hair and porcelain skin that can enable a woman to appear ageless. She began explaining her *Living with Momma* story by saying they had not made any rushed actions when considering this new lifestyle decision. There were many discussions, much advice sought, and more than a few prayers offered, even before Diane and her baby-boomer parents decided they would all leave their houses and move into one home together.

Diane had just been through a difficult divorce. Meanwhile, her father was diagnosed with cancer, and her mother was needing more help with the heavy physical side of his everyday recovery. Diane, and her two teen-aged sons, agreed they could be more helpful if they lived together with her parents. They also saw that combining all the basic living expenses from two households into one would help Diane contribute to the boys' impending college expenses while still paying down the debt her ex-husband had left her with, when he bailed on the family.

The house they found allowed her parents privacy in the converted walkout-level basement (mother-in-law suite). Diane and her boys lived on the first two floors. Even though there was a small kitchen in the basement, the whole family often shared the main kitchen and family room because Diane's mom enjoyed cooking and had agreed to prepare four meals a week. The boys enjoyed hanging out with their grandparents and all the benefits of coming home to a full house rather than an empty one while their mom was at work.

Diane's *best thing about living with her parents* was being able to watch the "tender moments of a long-term love" that her parents showed each other during her father's illness. She considered it healing, on many levels, after coming out of her messy relationship. She was proud that they were all making the new living arrangements work.

The one thing Diane wished she had known before they all moved in together was how far it would drive a wedge between her and her older sister, Jean. Her sister was a stay-at-home mom who had agreed to help their mom with some of the afternoon caretaker tasks (eg. doctors visits, rehab, or just light grocery shopping). There was a schedule posted on the fridge, so Diane usually knew when Jean had been to the house to help her mom and dad. Because everything was done in shifts, Diane hardly would spend any time with her sister, Jean, even though they were both taking care of the same people.

After one of the rehab visits, the two sisters hit a tipping point. Diane came home from work to find their mom sitting at the kitchen table silently crying and her sister standing by the stove with her brow furrowed and arms crossed. Jean barked, "Diane, Mom needs to face reality and start thinking about what she is going to do when Dad dies."

Diane blew her top. She barked right back. "D***, Jean, just stop coming over if all you are going to do is be so mean to Mom."

"You want that, don't you," Jean screamed, "since you already own everything that Mom and Dad have!" Then she walked out the door.

The sisters had not spoken since the blow-up. The "perfect arrangement" had begun showing its flaws (or claws). It's in those flaws that a "what if" monster appeared to Diane and she came to see me. I have seen the "what if" thoughts begin to seed havoc and consume a person or even whole families when it takes hold of our thoughts. Before we spoke, Diane obsessed over questions like, "*What if* the next time Jean and I talk another fight happens? *What if* a fight happens in front of our friends or extended family? *What if* we never talk again? *What if* Jean was right and mom wants to move out after dad dies?" What if, what if, what if?

'Be kind whenever possible. It is always possible.'

In the last chapter we discussed how you can (re)tell a story from the perspective of the fruits of love and peace. In Diane's narrative, we have *at least* six people living with the heightened emotions of a terminal illness and undiscussed adult sibling rivalry in a multi-generational house. How can we even begin to rewrite a story that includes all of those people? Often, having multiple caretaker stories might make us decide to go on autopilot, or go with the flow, as it were. But that is where the "what if" monster can control the actions of each person who is not brave enough to face their fear-filled thoughts with integrity. Why integrity? Because that is the special sauce we can use to make family relationships solid and whole. It opens up the possibilities for where we can be kind and good whenever possible. Or as the Dalai Lama would say. Kindness is always possible. A practical theologian would say since both Kindness and Goodness already have been given to us as promised fruit, let's eat some of divine fruit waiting to be enjoyed!

The most heartbreaking part of my ministry as a former hospital chaplain was being with families who were trying to make decisions and assume roles that had been forced on them by a terminal illness or a tragic accident. Often families had no idea how to even be kind or civil to each other in normal circumstances and then they were forced to work together in a time of trauma. Wow, let's just say it was hard on them. So often nurses paged me, not to support a patient, but to help the patient's *family* to calm down. The trauma of a hospital setting sends some family members into an emotional abyss. Their family integrity was just too weak to control the what-ifs with actions in union with the values and principles they often claimed to hold in non-stressful situations.

When the What-Ifs Take Control of a Family

The trouble between Diane and Jean had exposed several weaknesses in their seemingly perfect arrangement as loving people who wanted to care for their aging parents.. They had failed to discuss how the parents' "stuff" would be distributed after Mom and Dad both passed away; currently, everything was seemingly in one child's possession.

Why should these siblings even think about their parents' stuff, or the living arrangements anyway? Isn't that morbid or wouldn't it sound greedy? Not if they came together to discuss these real life issues in an effort to transplant new adult relationships in the place of childhood roles and rules that are outdated and unhealthy for any adult siblings to hold.

Financial experts contend that there are three common disagreements among adult siblings concerning their parents' finances: (1) how an inheritance will be divided; (2) whether one sibling supports the parents more than the other siblings; and (3) whether the parents are being fair in their financial support of their children.

These same experts are saying that siblings fighting over money or possessions is exactly what baby-boomer parents do *not* want to happen. However, avoiding the necessary conversations as a way to keep the peace is wishful thinking. Remaining silent can, and often does, become a powder keg waiting for a spark in many multi-generational family homes as well as with the family members who do not live in the same space. It's the proverbial "a goal without a plan is then nothing more than a wish." My grandfather would often say, "wish in one hand and crap in the other, then tell me which one fills up the fastest." As a kid I would just laugh when he said that. Mostly because crap was a funny word back then. Now as an adult it makes me sad. Maybe, that is because I have seen how much of that crap "hits the fan" when families are in a hospital room and don't know how to be kind to each other.

This is not a critique of Diane's family. They had done a really good job of assigning roles based on each person's unique circumstances and skills. But they all became busy in those caretaker roles and forgot to nourish their caregiver spirits in the process. They had not considered how important it was to set aside time with the whole family (not just those living together) to discuss openly how things were going and what needs were changing or needed to be addressed as time progressed. It seems very few people realize it is crucial to make time to talk about money and ensure everyone has a voice. You could do this at a family gathering on a set date, or, if you do not want to make one person be in charge of these discussions, consider having a professional mediate your gatherings.

Talking about key financial issues that need to be resolved reduces the "what if" worries that threaten family relationships. For example, you can discuss with your siblings how to pitch in to help an aging parent so that the largest portion does not fall on the one who lives the closest. There are many ways out-of-town siblings can contribute, such as paying for a monthly cleaning service and doing repair work around the house when visiting. Siblings must also talk about the non-financial responsibilities, so those do not fall disproportionately on one family member. Experts are telling us that one person (usually the oldest or closest living relative) is taking on more than 80% of the caretaking responsibilities. This is a leading cause of family discord as parents age and need help from their family members.

Avoiding inheritance blowups can be tricky. Being mindful of preventing future grudges over inheritances is a good place to start. In a best-case scenario, parents and adult children can sit down and talk openly about the plans parents have made and designate, in writing, who gets what. Research shows that most people who want to leave an inheritance to children or grandchildren have not told them what to expect. If your parents are not sure (for whatever reason) if they want to discuss this in detail with the family, ask them to work with an attorney to make a will and to add a companion document which explains their rationale. Giving everyone a copy of this document can help reduce the guessing that fuels the rancor of sibling rivalry while grieving lost parents. Let your parents know that all their children are working together to care for them and want to honor them in the same way after they are gone.

'How you love anything is how you love everything'
Richard Rohr says, in his book *Yes…And*, a truth that is both complicated and simple: "How you love anything is how you love everything. Love is a quality of relationship more than a statement about the worthiness or deservedness of the object loved."

This truth can lead our caregiver selves to **think** with the integrity of goodness and our caretaker selves to **act** with integrity of goodness. What is LIVING a Good Life with the Integrity of Goodness? It is our ability to encourage with an honesty that avoids all forms of harshness or cruelty by holding others in high esteem. To get this definition, I had to start with our earliest definitions of the words to get a richer and more ripe meaning for our fruits of goodness and kindness.

The English language doesn't have a word that carries quite the notion of what goodness means in Hebrew and Aramaic. The Hebrew definition of *goodness* overlaps with the Greek word for *kindness* and means "meeting a need" or "avoiding harshness or cruelty." Merriam-Webster's claims that *goodness* refers to the character traits such as integrity, honesty, encouragement, and "conduct that entitles a person to high esteem," while kindness is a quality of being generous, considerate, and treating people with respect. Although they are defined slightly differently, put into action they can be used synonymously. Consider, for example, interchanging "the quality of the relationship" with the words *love, goodness, kindness,* and *mercy* (Luke 6:35–36).

A spiritual example of what goodness/kindness looks like is found in the parable of the prodigal son (Luke 15:11–32). I think this passage should be renamed "the parable of the prodigal's father." Please read the entire passage from the Book of Luke yourself. I suggest that essentially, it describes a family squabble involving sibling rivalry and people who have misaligned intentions. In short, it sounds like this:

One son says, "Give me my share."

The other son says, "What about me?"

When we analyze this passage using practical theology, we can ask, "How am *I* like these people or characters in this story?" Respectfully, we can see that these two competing sons could be any one of us. When we are truthful with ourselves, we can see that *we are both of them*. I confess to times of feeling envious of a family member or refusing to acknowledge that I am not better than anyone else. There were times when I did not appreciate what my family had given me or when I have been just plain stupid with money. It's not that hard to confess or bore others with my personal weaknesses concerning my own family of origin. That is the past. Reflection is easier in that space. What I need to do is have the integrity, which takes courage, to see how I have perpetuated these weakness in my present family.

Children Start Off by Comparing— It's Simply One Way to Learn

The brothers in this parable could be *any* child I have ever met. The "give me my share/what about me" attitude reminds me of times that I'd serve a special dessert to my own children. I would cut pieces of cake for my three daughters, and no matter how old they were, they all watched with critical intent to make sure each of them got the piece that was the same size as their sibling. I have even seen this behavior in babies as young as six months. For example, babies want to eat off of their mother's plate even when they have the same food sitting right in front of them. This is normal human behavior. Other people provided us with food when we were young and fed us directly by hand or breast, illustrating a comparison dynamic which is written deep in our DNA. That said, most of the time my daughters were excited to get a slice of cake, other times their smiles would disappear and I would hear the awful "her piece is bigger" complaint.

As a parent, when we hear the dreaded me-me-me, mine-mine-mine statements from one of our children, we may feel like we are not very good parents. Sometimes, when my children threw these guilt provoking comparisons around it made me feel like I was trying to nail Jell-O to the wall. How does a person respond when accused (even by a toddler) of being "more giving" to one child over another? It can spark emotions straight from our own childhood, right?

At such times, I would have to remind myself that the issue was really about a piece of cake, not all the deep-seated emotions of trying to be a perfect parent. It is just about a piece of cake and not the impossible task of "making" our children feel a certain way. If I did not stay aware of the real issue, then a seemingly selfish demand from my children could trigger unkind words to spew from my mouth (read: guilt or shame statements like "Why don't you be grateful?" "Just be happy with what you have." "Don't you know how hard I work?" and other poorly considered, social and culturally ingrained shame or guilt lessons).

Still, over the years, my husband and I constantly tried new ideas to move our children out of that "her piece is bigger" attitude. In the long run, it was up to my adult daughters to choose to practice behaviors and attitudes that were less competitive with their siblings; I cannot fix my adult children. Remember, we have already discussed that Jesus isn't going to "fix" family members to suit our standards of conduct either. If my husband and I are still trying to model behavior that is kind and compassionate around our children, but then we fall short when we are not intentionally acting with integrity in the spirit of compassion, we need to stop and redirect ourselves with integrity. Like the integrity modeled in the story of the father of the prodigal son so richly displayed with his patience, kindness, and gentle actions.

Integrity of Goodness in Action

Few people impart wisdom or compassion through storytelling as well as the Dalai Lama. He tells us that "the purpose of all major religious traditions is not to construct big temples on the outside, but to create temples of goodness and compassion on the inside of our hearts." In his book *A Force for Good*, in collaboration with Daniel Goleman, he explains how we can turn our compassionate energy outward in the form of goodness. Harnessing good actions produces positive energy for ourselves and meaningful effects in the larger world.

So, let's get back to the parable of the prodigal son's father. No matter what his sons demanded of him, he did not get angry, did not keep a record of wrongs, was patient, was kind, and was not self-seeking in his responses. Sounds like the 1 Corinthians definition of love, doesn't it? Somehow, right in the middle of all the hoopla, the father remains good and kind. He is not harsh, he is not cruel, and he looks at his misguided sons with compassion. Sounds like that father is full of divine fruit. Some even say that the father in this parable represents the Creator, but I am wary of that idea because that can make it difficult to see that this is an achievable human state.

Jane, one of my dearest friends' took the responsibility to acknowledge the fruit of kindness and goodness with the brave actions of a peace-filled love toward her own siblings, during the aging of her parents. She told me of a situation that was similar to Diane's and Jean's angry fight and what-if thoughts. Jane's fight with her sister started shortly after their mother's death. It was scary and hard for my friend even to recount this story, but she gave me permission to repeat it so that others could see how a family can have ever-growing fruitful relationships by facing some of our own "what if" monsters:

Mom's Alzheimer's finally got so bad that we had to put her in a facility for her last six months. My sisters and I had to make that decision. Even though one of my sisters has worked in healthcare institutions and served in nursing homes for most of her career, it was still hard to decide what was best for our mother. We couldn't take care of her well medically anymore. The strokes that Dad had suffered made it so he did not understand why Mom had to go to the nursing home. He still doesn't.

It was just after we put mom in the nursing home that my sister and I got into a huge fight. It was like reliving our teenage years all over again. Back then, we had shared a room, but we were so different. She was an extrovert. I was an introvert. We did not hang out with the same people. I would dare to say that we hated each other a little bit as teenagers. So, when we had a fight about the care of our parents it was horrid. Screaming. Throwing things. The only thing that got us to the other side was our mother.

When we were growing up and we fought, our mother made us work it out. Mother had been raised in a family where the siblings had fought years before, and they had not spoken to each other for years since. They were dying off and still not speaking to each other. Mother made us "just keep talking." She told us, "Whatever you do, you cannot stop talking." So we kept talking. And I am so glad that we lived that advice. Because being able to share in caring for our parents with my sisters has been deeply moving. We have lost mom, for now, but not each other.

Displaying the qualities of the fruit of goodness and kindness in a family full of caregivers could be a perfect solution to many of our social problems. But learning to push through our emotions with the integrity to purposefully include everyone equally takes on challenges that we may not see coming—until they do. This is where professional lawyers, accountants, ministers, and even people now trained as geriatric counselors can come in to help us keep everyone in the caretaker arena up to date on the details (with deep emotional roots) surrounding aging parents.

Suggested Exercises

The following exercises take a different form from those in the previous three chapters. Hopefully by now you are writing your answers in your notebook or journal in whatever form that is driving your own journey through this book.

Diane, whom we met in this chapter, was having a hard time translating what she wished she had known before she moved in with her parents, namely, how it would jeopardize her relationship with her sister, Jean. She sought counseling that addressed the specifics of her "what if" monsters. She gave herself a safe space to let go of the trauma of old personal wounds and the harmful patterns caused by years of fighting with her sister. Diane found those spaces by choosing to begin her own journey into integrity of kindness/goodness.

I suggested the following exercise, to Diane, to create a safe space for personal healing from the emotional trauma of fighting with a family member or a loved one in general.

I have done this exercise on many occasions myself. It has helped me regain a sense of seeing "the other" with eyes of kindness and goodness. It is a reset button for our heart in those times when we feel weakest and need help clearing our view—or harsh opinions—toward someone who has hurt us. I call this exercise "Let Me Count the Ways."

You will actually be counting fifty ways (or reasons) you love someone. This directs your vision back to what the sacred texts teach is divine kindness reflected in our human experience. Expressing kindness to our family can be a ritual to, with, for and in our Creator (Matt. 9:13, 12:7). How? We can begin to reflect on the character and virtues shown by the father of the prodigal son. His integrity showed kindness and goodness that never depended on the other person acting in "the right way."

1. On a piece of paper write the numbers 1 through 50 near the left margin.
2. At the top of the paper write the name of a person you are having a really hard time showing or even having loving feelings toward. Keep this simple and think about only one person at a time.
3. Think of things this person does or has a way of being that you enjoy, like, or admire. Fill out all 50 spaces on the list with the ways you enjoy, celebrate, admire this person whose name you wrote at the top of the page. Be specific. Do not list superficial traits, e.g., "I like the dress Jenny has on today." Instead, think of the fundamental reason behind the thing you enjoy, such as "Jenny has a wonderful sense of style." It will not do your heart good to write things that are not in "Jenny's" control, e.g., "Jenny is pretty," that is something she inherited from DNA.

While it may sound like there are too many rules to do this exercise well, I must tell you that rules are not the hard part of this exercise. If you are mad, the hardest part is writing even the first three things you admire or like about the person you are feeling negative about! I promise you, it will get easier. I also promise you it will get hard, again, when you reach about twenty. This is when most people want to quit. Wherever it gets to be the most difficult, that is when you must open your heart the most. When you are finished, review your list and let your caring self feel the goodness in that person.

One time I was so angry about a situation between me and a family member I had to carry my empty "Let Me Count the Ways" list for a whole week before I could wrap my heart around appreciating (what was good in) that person. I filled the first space with something like, "she is not mean to everyone, just me." Yeah, that didn't work out well. I had to erase that passive-aggressive compliment and start over. If you don't know what a passive-aggressive compliment is, it is when someone tells you something nice about yourself but it makes you feel like you did something wrong or stupid or silly instead. In the South, those "nice compliments" usually begin with the saying: "Well, bless her heart…"

As before, I urge you, if there is any chemical or physical abuse in a relationship, seek professional help because these exercises are designed for healing, *not* for escaping from abusive situations.

Chapter 5

Valuing Patience

"*Patience is the training in abiding with the restlessness of our energy and letting things evolve at their own speed.*"
— **Pema Chödrön,** American Tibetan Buddhist Nun

"*To learn patience is not to rebel against every hardship.*"
— **Henri Nouwen,** Dutch priest, professor, and writer

"*Be patient toward all that is unsolved in your heart and try to love the questions themselves.*"
— **Rainer Maria Rilke,** Poet and novelist

T he first time I met Betsy, age fifty-five, she was wearing a dark green sweater that was so bedazzled and glittery that in the right light she might have been mistaken for a walking Christmas tree. If I narrowed my eyes and looked just past her, her perfectly styled silver hair could have been the star. She opened a purse so full it made a clunking sound when she set it on the floor and pulled out an eight-by-ten day planner that was color-coded and sectioned off for home, classroom, and projects. I was feeling a little green, myself (with envy) because in my wildest dreams I could never be so organized. I longed to sit at her feet and learn from this master planner guru.

Betsy wanted to discuss the issues she was having with her father. She knew he was a "stubborn old goat" before she and her husband offered for him to move in. She loved her father, but he was driving her crazy. His demands for attention made her feel like she could not please him. She also had a husband and two boys at home waiting for her attention.. In addition to these heavy demands, Betsy was concerned that her father was showing signs of Alzheimer's. He refused to let Betsy talk to the doctor without him being in the room, and she believed she just "couldn't say her concerns in front of him!"

The Billy Goat Song

Studies at the New Jersey Institute for Successful Aging found that members of the sandwich generation report instances when their aging parents are "acting in ways that are commonly attributed to stubbornness." Some experts claimed stubbornness might be a symptom of an older person's struggle to maintain independence or a breakdown in communication between the generations. Older adults try to preserve the life they had and the people they were before they aged. This is not a new issue but is being studied more frequently with our aging population. That said, the goal is to understand "perceptions of older parents and their adult children regarding behavior that is perceived to be stubborn" in order to find better ways to have important conversations.

For early baby-boomer parents to respond positively to advice or help, those of us in the sandwich generation must learn new ways to communicate what is important. If an aging parent insists, resists, or persists in doing things their own way, which risks their health or the well-being of others, then what? Who tells Dad that it's time to give up his car keys and what can be done if he refuses? How do we get Mom to take her medication when she thinks she has but we know she hasn't?

Letting Things Evolve

Okay, we may think we understand that many people over seventy are concerned with losing control in their lives and their diminishing independence. But research uncovers a huge paradox in this area: parents are both annoyed by their children's advice and feel more loved by their concerns. Further complicating learning to care for our parents is the struggle to know whether our aging parent is still capable of making good, sound decisions. This struggle can eventually allow us to fall into an abyss of a codependent role where we are parenting our parents. This *never* works out well in the long run. We can easily become afraid when our parent's health starts to show signs of aging, and it can be hard for us to let life evolve as it should. We also can become less patient with them. At times we become less patient with our own aging process when we are watching our parents age (sometimes rapidly) right before our very eyes.

In Betsy's situation, codependency flags started to wave when Betsy's father, Ben (age eighty-one), came to me to discuss living with his daughter. He started our talk by explaining that he only came to me because of Betsy's insistence. He made it known straight away that he was "not very keen on this meeting." I chose to ignore his passive aggressive swipe at his daughter and counseling in-general and concentrated on how much of a doppelgänger to an older Jack Nicholson he was, and as I looked into the soft, blue, soulful eyes of the man sitting in front of me I began with the question, "Tell me about how you came to be living within the same home as your adult daughter."

Here is a condensed version of Ben's story: After retiring from an upper-level executive position at a national phone company, he and his wife, Liz, enjoyed a few years traveling together and spending evenings with friends. Their lives had become everything they had hoped for over their years together.

When Liz's cancer returned after ten years in remission, it was a difficult and all-consuming year because the disease spread so fast. After Liz passed, Ben spent a couple of years staying close to home, trying to figure out what to do next since everything he had known (work, marriage, and adult children) was no longer part of his daily life. One day, he fell off a ladder while fixing a gutter on the house. He broke his ankle and bruised his self-sufficient pride. That was when his daughters offered for him to stay with them during his recovery, and he struggled with the decision to do so. He did not want to choose which daughter to live with. Wouldn't one of them feel left out or, worse, less loved? "They" decided that Ben should consider living full-time with Betsy's family during the fall and winter seasons and with Kay's family in the spring and summer months. He put the house on the market and made the leap.

Identifying Matters of the Heart

Ben admitted that this first year with his daughter Betsy's family had some challenges but overall it was good. He was able to spend time getting to know his grandchildren better because it had mainly been his wife's role to tell him how everyone was doing. While Ben admitted that Betsy insisted he come to talk about living together, he did, however, have an opinion he wanted to discuss which was his response to "what is the one thing you wish you knew before moving in with…" I had him answer before our meeting.

Ben wished he knew *how long it was going to take to sell his house*. It had been over 9 months and it had not sold. In retrospect, he thought that maybe not selling his house may have been a blessing. Why? Because he was considering moving back into it now that his ankle was all better.

Ben then paused and looked at me. I think he was expecting advice. I don't really work that way. Instead I asked Ben if he could tell me, in one sentence, why he wanted to move back into his house now that his ankle was better. He looked down and said, "I am lonely and I want to go home."

The one thing Ben wished he knew before he moved in with his adult children was how "lonely" it would make him feel. How could that be? He was surrounded by family. He didn't want to hurt their feelings, but his daughters and their husbands made him feel old. Really old. "Whenever they catch me in a memory lapse (like not knowing the name of an object) they exchange these long looks. Their scrutiny is making me so self-conscious. Everyone has those moments when they forget why the walked into a room, right? I am finding myself making excuses, so I don't have to be in the same room with both of them."

Even When Being Loved We Can Still Feel Lonely

Although researchers are still piecing together what exactly happens in a healthy aging brain, they are beginning to map out the typical memory changes of aging. The National Institute on Aging, working with researchers in this field, views memory change "as a collection of specific and only subtle changes." This can help erase the gloomy stereotype about us all "losing it" with age. Moreover, when aging adults experience a slowing or loss of cognitive function, it can make them depressed. They might then lose interest in everyday activities and events that help maintain and strengthen cognitive functioning. It's a bitter circle.

Aging research shows that reducing anxiety (a precursor to some forms of depression) can help people learn and remember more efficiently. Researchers also have found that when people think they can do it—a concept known as self-efficacy—they actually perform better on tests. People of all ages can demonstrate self-efficacy. For example, students who tested in subjects they feel they are good at actually score better than when they are tested in subjects they feel are hard. Optimism, self-belief, and self-efficacy are ways we view ourselves and the choices and decisions we make.

We in the sandwich generation must be aware that, as our roles shift to caring for our own former caregivers, we must help our aging parents preserve their sense of self-efficacy. How can we help them preserve their sense of self-worth? An important mantra to remember is: Don't become our parents' parents—when we do, we remove yet another role that aging has naturally taken from them.

One way to make sure we are not falling into parenting our parents is to treat them like they are essential to the family's well-being. This ability to value something or someone is essential, as more of the population moves into the age bracket associated with higher rates of mild cognitive impairment. What we may first perceive as stubbornness in our aging parents is likely linked to how we are managing our relationships. For example, after being diagnosed with ALS, Richard Glatzer wrote the movie *Still Alice* based on neurologist Lisa Genova's best selling novel of the same name. In the novel the linguistics professor Alice Howland received a diagnosis of early-onset Alzheimer's disease. Genova wrote the inspiring book *Still Alice* about how family's bonds were thoroughly tested and the efforts they made to stay connected to "who she once was." Alice lived a story in which she chose to lean in where most of us would rather have collapsed or even backed away.

Her novel is a great example of spiritual listening and being patient with a person, not distracted by the fears that naturally occur when a family member experiences memory loss. It's said that "patience is not the ability to wait but how you act while you're waiting." Looking at this role reversal with eyes that value patience may help us avoid being a caretaker who is demeaning or who treats our parents like they are children.

Valuing Patience

Our caregiver selves can value the patience as necessary for replacing frustrations and fears that naturally creep up on us as we worry about our parents' safety in their independence. Fear is one of the first emotions to be challenged when welcoming the fruit that comes in the form of patience. I don't know about you, but one of the only things that scared me as much as seeing my two-year-old teetering at the top of rickety-rusty slide (she had somehow scrambled up without me seeing her) was seeing my father, more than seventy years old, on top of a rickety-ladder trying to paint a window ledge, because he "had never paid anybody to paint his house and he wasn't going to start now." What do we do when we see our parents making poor choices? If we let fear take over and we scream, "Get down from there" they could fall. So, we have to be patient, and consciously calm, and still get them safely down. Getting them to come down safely needs to happen immediately. We need to help them without being over excited or angry (anger is usually just a reaction to fear) if we want the best results for their safety, right?

The Hebrew concept of patience is found all over Judeo-Christian scriptures. One of the oldest being a sense of forbearance, or yielding when offended and being (very) slow to anger. I love the Hebrew idiom of patience; that being a picture of the "slow venting of air through the nostrils." This characteristic of being slow to anger and blowing air out of my nose implies someone who is not easily offended or fearfully driven by actions of others.

Although most people today consider patience to be passive waiting, or gentle tolerance, the Greek words for patience are actually very active, robust words. So while patience is an action: *to wait*, it is also just as importantly *to hope for* and *to continue to have faith* in a higher purpose, like those found woven throughout the books of Ecclesiastes.

This then brings us to our larger view and broader definition of Valuing Patience—which will allow us to enjoy *LIVING* a good life— Valuing Patience is having a high opinion or respecting someone by yielding to the benefits of hope despite their actions. This new concept of patience is important in our lives in the sandwich generation. When we can open our caregiver self to feast on the fruit of patience, as a practical truth, we can get our children and our parents off of the rickety spaces (that could be harmful) with confidence in both themselves and ourselves.

Patience can help renew our steadfast spirits so we can act lovingly towards the people we love. We can then also be willing to see the natural and normal stages of aging with empathy as a good first step toward patience. Empathy is when we can put ourselves in another person's shoes, or to imagine experiencing what others are experiencing. It is extremely important to note that empathy *is not* sympathy, pity, or allowing emotions like fear, shame, or unexplored guilt to cause you "fix things" or "help" more frequently than is good for you or them. A person full of empathy will bring a connection and a bond to a relationship. A person full of pity will to attempt control "the problem" which removes connections within relationships. No one is helpless and no one wants to feel helpless either.

Sometimes practicing patience can be highly charged because it is difficult to empathize with a parent who only wants to talk about how hard life is, how sick they are, or how no one ever pays them any attention. Some experts contend that it is hard to fulfill the demands imposed on us when our empathetic nature meshes with our sympathetic nature.

When we feel we are being given demands we *do* something we get worn out. Maybe, to much sympathy instead of healthy connections found in empathy is why we feel it is an obligation to help since they are family.

In Betsy and Ben's situation, I offered them a way to develop more empathy towards each other with a new mindset of active patience. I have used this exercise myself often. Why? Over the years I have had to consider many dilemmas (such as with my father on the ladder) and find ways to express empathy, in a healthy way, toward my own aging parents and adult children. First, I ask myself to imagine that I have grown old. Then, from the perspective of my being more than ninety years old, I imagine looking back to my present life and ask myself to consider whether there is anything I will regret about the decisions or actions I am making right now. Another thing I do to feel patient when making decisions and choices for myself or others (especially concerning my adult children) is I will write out what my dream or ideal life with them could/would look like if I could predict it over the next year.

Everyone has dreams. For example, people have wishes, prayers, and hopes for their children all the time. However, I suggest that few people have dreamed about what a good life looks like *with* their aging parent. Or what their dream life would look like *with* an adult child. I am going to assume that most of us have probably never asked our parents or our grown children to tell us about their *own* dreams in/for their lives. Why do we stop asking people what they want to be when they grow up when they reach a certain age? I suggest, dreaming together with our families looks different than dreaming alone.

Dreaming together sounded like a good idea to both Ben and his daughters. They decided to use it as a way to start their individual and combined journeys into being more patient with each other. Here's their version: They each spent time alone writing down a dream (and a goal) for their own lives that could happen within the next year. Because everyone was willing to listen with empathy—patiently, not allowing anger, not being offended, not judging how are what was said, by what anyone may have dreamed—they then came together to read their dreams out loud. By agreeing to listen and not react to what was being read out loud, they created a unified safe space to tell their most vulnerable wishes.

A few things rose to the surface within this patient space for Ben and his family. They all were able to look at living together from a fresh point of view. They did not allow the assumptions or the fears to take over the conversations. They learned to be less afraid and to rely on each other instead of "fixing each other." They all agreed they had good intentions but the many unspoken fears and "what if's" had led to poor results.

By listening to everyone's dream instead of rehashing the nightmares that came with the "what if'" monsters they were able to consider collectively what was best for them as a family. Most important to the dream was the adult action that followed: they all acknowledged still being raw from the death of their mother/wife and were then able to see where grief had discolored some of the previous decisions and attitudes that had occurred between them. They each had spent time stating a dream for the next year in three sentences.

Here were their collective dreams in the briefest form:

Valuing patience allowed Ben to tell his daughters he wanted friends his own age to spend time with. Betsy wanted to have a relationship with her dad, but not one where she only spent time with him as a caretaker out of guilt, because her mother was gone. Betsy's husband and her sister both joined the discussion, and they had similar dreams but mainly they all wanted quality time with each other.

They considered the value in these ideal dreams and together they came up with the idea to look into other options for living that included as many of their goals as possible. Ben had the financial means, even before his house was sold, to live in a community of retired people his own age. They decided to look at independent living communities together and found one that met his budget, which offered activities for people his age, and even had options for future health care needs should they be necessary. Even better, the one community they liked the most was a ten-minute drive to Betsy's house. Ben could still spend time with both daughters and even more with his grandchildren, yet he could also find friends his own age, and activities to occupy his thoughts and time. It was a win-win for everyone. That is what happens when a seed of the fruit given by the Spirit falls on good soil (Luke 8:1–13).

Suggested Exercises

1. Breathe deeply. Breathe in as you silently count to eight. Hold your breath for a heartbeat or a count of two. Then slowly exhale as you count to eight. Repeat three times.

2. Plan on doing this three times each day. Deep breathing like this reduces stress and can even improve your memory.

3. Reflect on Luke 8:1-13. What could happen if the seed of the fruit given by the Spirit falls on good soil?

4. Rethinking instant gratification. We have inherited a desire for instant gratification from a culture of constant choices, non-stop media, and unconscious input from living in a commercially driven society. Did you know that people actually pay money for silence? It is called a vacation. Plan one, even if you can't take it right away, planning a vacation can be fun and will give you a positive goal to work towards.

5. In this exercise, you will take a free mini vacation into a world of media silence. Choose one day to turn off the TV, radio, cell phone, and computer. That also means ignoring newspapers and magazines too. Wait, what? Even magazines? Yep, consider this a break from being told everything you need to do to be happy, healthy, wealthy, and wise. For one whole day, take a

vacation from the media that causes you (unconscious) stress by insisting on projects to be done and purchases to be made.

Journal what you do instead during your media vacation time and how it affects you. Decide if and how you can do this at least once a month. Work your way up to three media vacation days a month, and journal about what you see and do without all the noise telling you what to think.

6. Find someone in your family who is willing to dream with you. Each of you write down a dream or a goal that you have for yourself that could happen in the next year. Read your answers out loud. Practice listening by spending time hearing them and asking open-ended questions to get to know each other better.

Chapter 6

Insightful Self-Control

"A parable calls us to insight and decision. A parable doesn't lead us to more mental analysis; it's either a flashing insight or it's nothing. It calls us more to decision and a change of perspective."
– Richard Rohr, Yes…And

"I did not know that help is the sunny side of control… But now I know that it is defeating and abusive to try and get people to do what I was sure would help them."
– Anne Lamott, Novelist and non-fiction writer

"I think we lost touch with the idea that speaking honestly and openly about who we are, about what we are feeling, and about our experiences (good and bad) is the definition of courage."
– Brené Brown, The Gifts of Imperfection

Connie was concerned about her sister's dementia. She was afraid it was worse than the doctor would acknowledge. Connie and her sister Macie were best friends, but they had not been spending as much time together since Macie's son Jack had moved back home with his mother, after his divorce. What was pushing her concerns for her sister was how she had to insist Macie see a doctor after complaining of shortness of breath. At at that appointment they discovered that Macie had two cracked ribs yet she did not remember falling.

In addition, it seemed like Macie was not staying on top of other things like paying her bills. When they went to lunch, her sister's credit card was declined at the table so Connie took care of the check. She didn't mind helping—she loved being able to buy a meal for her sister—but this was just not like Macie. She was usually the organized one in the family.

Around the time when Connie spoke with me about Macie's situation I had set up a working lunch with my friend Sandy. Sandy had recently bought into a franchise offering home-care services. This was not the first business that she had owned; she had made a considerable amount of money "seeing the market" over the years. Sandy was one of the most business-savvy women I knew *and* one of the funniest people I have ever met. I was looking forward to time with her because I knew I could ask her anything and did not have to temper my curiosity. She would not only be honest but also bring some humor into my research on home care services and baby boomers.

Aging in the 21st Century

I knew from a previous conversation that Sandy's home care business was already making a profit, which is another reason I set up the lunch date. I wanted to know what was working and what was problematic in this industry. I opened our conversation with a question I thought would set a positive tone for our discussion. "What is the one thing that has surprised you the most about your new business?"

Her response knocked the wind right out of me. Her cheeks flamed red, and she told me, "I never knew how many family members are physically harming their aging relatives." Sandy admitted she was filing a new abuse report almost every month. "This was not what I expected at all."

Sandy also discovered the person who was being abused rarely admitted it, therefore it took a long time for a case of abuse to be proved. She was forced to establish several new policies to protect her staff and her clients for those reasons. Her new policies demanded honesty with all employees and clients and made it mandatory to tell her if *any* abuse was suspected in the home. She enforced the honesty policies which immediately removed her staff from the clients' homes and reported the abuse to the authorities. Sandy rarely heard whether anyone was charged with a crime or if the abuse ended once her staff left the homes. Sandy and her clients reside in a state with mandated reporting requirements (under the Elder Abuse Victims Act of 2009) which help protect older adults. This mandate requires all medical professionals or anyone responsible for the care of an elderly person to file a report on suspected abuse.

We have all heard stories about nursing homes or hired staff doing in-home care, being abusive. I did not realize that family members were also frequently suspected. According to the 2010 U.S. Census, the United States has the greatest number and proportion of people older than sixty-five since our census began. Currently, 40.3 million people (13 percent of the population) are baby boomers or members of Generation X, and it is predicted that by 2050 the number of older adults will double to over 83 million people. As early as 2030, there will be more than 8.9 million people in the oldest age group, those eighty-five years old and older.

A study of 4,156 older adults by the National Center on Elder Abuse (NCEA) suggests that the most common perpetrators of financial exploitation of older adults *are family members* (57.9 percent), followed by friends and neighbors (16.9 percent) and home care aides (14.9 percent). Another study compared 5,777 adults over the age of sixty across types of mistreatment. It suggests a "higher proportion of physical mistreatment" is perpetrated by people who had used or were using substances (alcohol or drugs) at the time of the incident, who lived with the victim, and who were related to the victim.

How Could Elder Abuse Happen so Often?

AARP is working on several fronts with both families and state legislatures "to preserve and strengthen" state adult protective services. Research shows that the majority of unconscionable abuse of our older parents, spouses, and other loved ones occurs right in the homes *where people want to be*. Visit the AARP website for resources on protecting our vulnerable older people: aarp.org/supportcaregivers.

I do not want to minimize the disgraceful behavior of elder abuse—people captive to alcoholism and drug addiction typically act morally bankrupt—but research is also showing another reason that the rate of elder abuse is rising. So many untrained family members provide the bulk of care for our oldest generations. How are ordinary people to know how to safely lift an aging person into a standing position with no one getting hurt? How do people know when their own thoughts are too scattered from sleep deprivation, related to caring for an aging parent, to make safe and sound decisions for the elder person in their care? How does caretaker fatigue affect the quality of care we provide our aging population?

Connie is not the only person I have spoken with who was concerned about the health of a family member and how they are beginning to suspect that another family member may be a cause for the concern.

I have spoken with several people who suspected abuse or caretaker fatigue in the home. Often they saw the concern in the form of neglect. How can we tell if there is abuse? How can we help if it is caretaker fatigue? Really, how do we even define the responsibilities of the people living with aging parents?

In one particular case, no one (else) in the family would acknowledge the horrid conditions other than Janet: Janet's elderly sister was diagnosed with dementia. For financial reasons she was living in the home of her daughter, who was the primary caretaker. Janet had chosen to stop visiting because she always wanted "to just scoop her up and take her home with her" but could not because of her own health issues. On her last visit, Janet had spent most of the time washing away the smell of urine that permeated everything. She tried to smile when her sister recounted a memory of when they were children together, but she was too distracted with sorrow to enjoy a walk down memory lane.

I told Janet about our state's elder abuse hotline and suggested she call a family meeting with her siblings to discuss her concerns. Collective family wisdom can be a strong force in combating abuse and identifying caretaker fatigue. She was extremely nervous about how the "family would react" if she reported anything to the authorities on the basis of just "her thoughts." She went from being concerned for her sister to "maybe my niece was just having a bad day or something." And even though she knew her niece had struggled with drugs in the past, Janet became "pretty sure that the drug problems were resolved now." She thought her niece was holding down a job and maybe she was "just tired."

To her credit, Janet did make the call to the elder abuse hotline. Tragically, this was only after she had confided in her best friend about calling social services and together they decided to keep it all confidential. She did not have a family meeting. She did not ask for help from the family at all. She figured, correctly, that she would get caught in the crosshairs if the family knew what she was going to call social-services so she chose to remain silent and hope for the best. But after a case worker unexpectedly showed up at her niece's home, the family gossip train took off from Rumor Mill Station and headed straight into Crazy Town. The "issue" of the secret reporter distracted everyone in the family (that were *now* involved) from the possibility that abuse was occurring. If she did not want to head up such a meeting (for whatever reason) then she could have received help from her pastor or a geriatric counselor being a mediator. There are many useful resources to promote understanding and knowledge on elder care within our own U.S. Administration on Aging including free downloads, booklets, and hotlines for up to date information.

Insightful Self-Control, Defined

Being insightful is when we are willing to gain clarity into a complex problem (like elder abuse) so we can better understand our obligation. It can then help us to respond to problems we must face with courage instead of fear.

The word *insight* represents the same concept in Hebrew as the words *discernment*, *intuition*, and *awareness*. In the Judeo-Christian context, gaining insight or a deep intuitive understanding of a person or event is often called discernment. Unfortunately, practicing discernment is one area where many (religious) people stumble. We get so caught up in understanding what infallible standards are, concerning scriptures, that our behavior becomes doctrinally directed rather than spiritually led. Even though many people consider discernment, even outside of scriptures, to be a virtue of an individual who possesses wisdom, often we avoid discerning or spiritual listening. We do this by using excuses that spiritual insights or discernment are just for the preachers, teachers, and theologians to think about.

The dictionary definition of *self-control* is "restraint exercised over one's impulses, emotions or desires." In Greek, it means modesty or temperance, and in Hebrew it means inner strength. Because it is clear in Galatians 5 that self-control is the inner gift of the Spirit, it must also be considered a gift of inner strength within our caregiver self. Some say self-control is the last in the list of gifts given and is a sort of summation of the other gifts and virtues. I suggest that when it is translated from the Aramaic texts, it has the same meaning as in 2 Peter 1, which claims self-control is a promise given to become more reverent in the power of a Creator God and *all that has been created.*

Therefore, our broader definition of Insightful Self-Control for *LIVING* is: the ability to discern when our impulses, desires, or emotions should be tempered by considering that people are made in the image of a Divine Creator. If someone is a child of the Creator, they are amazing, special, blessed and divine, right? Maybe we should all be spending a bit of time asking ourselves how we would actually speak, act, or even what activities we would choose to participate in, if we were sitting in a room full of people with the royal lineage of the very Creator of the Universe.

Productive Family Relationships

An issue like caregiver burnout requires time for rest and healing. Because you are reading this book, I assume that you are a caregiver (not an abuser). If you are tired or afflicted by caregiver fatigue, looking for your own fruit of insightful self-control can be discovered with the resources offered within this book and the accompanying website.

Exhausted caregivers seeking the fruit of self-control can use spiritual practices from many faith traditions. Silence, solitude, meditative prayer, and reflective listening are all being taught and practiced in mainline churches and synagogues. You do not need to be a member to use these resources. In these practices many are finding hope and identifying moral standards that support them in productive family relationships.

Yoga and mindfulness classes are offered in many libraries, YMCA's, and community centers for free.

Government websites provide excellent resources on preventing caretaker/caregiver burnout. I offer a small list where you can begin your search at my website www.worldpeaceproject.com. The website for AARP is one of my favorite sites for updated information on medical and emotional services concerning caregivers and our aging population.

Some people may want to invest in professional advice from an elder care mediator or take part in classes given by Programs of All-Inclusive Care for the Elderly (PACE). Many parks and recreation centers offer adult day care services, elderly exercise programs, and free lunches for aging people. They also hold classes (many free) to help caregivers identify when and how to get help with the constant care needs of aging parents.

If you are having a hard time getting or accepting help from your family members with caregiving, the resources above give you a beginning awareness of where to get support. First though, you should discern why you think you are the only one doing what needs to be done. Perhaps you reached out a hand for help and support in the past but lack of response made you feel like you drew back a bloody stump. Perhaps that pain stems from feeling minimized or belittled or ignored, and you told yourself it is easier to go it alone. When we try to self-protect because of past trauma, it leaves us feeling like asking for help is just one more thing we have no control over.

When you realize you do have more options (physically and spiritually) from outside resources, you may find the courage to listen to some spiritual insight of self-control—which you already possess but must remember is waiting to connect to your tired caretaker self. I am going to tell you how my insight showed up when I needed it the most. Remember the story I told in Chapter 2 about falling asleep in the McDonald's parking lot? Well… I didn't exactly tell you the whole story.

A Rollercoaster Ride Powered by 'Yes' Guilt

As I mentioned, at that time, my husband and I were trapped in the middle of "doing good" with our caretaker selves. We just kept on saying "yes" to our loved ones' perceived next needs. I say perceived because most of the time they never asked for help; they would just simply tell us a problem and we would jump to rescue or help. We were not even stopping to think or weigh any long-term consequences to our actions. We were too blinded by what I call "yes guilt." *Yes guilt* is when we see no other choices than to say yes to others' needs—because we could only see these needs as our obligations to the family. Otherwise known as "that's just what family does" syndrome.

These were the false obligations—classically conditioned into us—as parents who had never really allowed our children to act like adult-children, nor our own parents to act like the adults they still were (even when they became frail). We were guilty of holding onto our relationships as codependents who were not conscious of how "helping" or being good "nurturing" parents was negatively affecting the people we loved the most. We were living as though in order for us to be able to have mutually satisfying relationships with our family members, (especially as they left the nest or suffered with an illness) it was okay for them to act clingy or unaccountable (read: helpless) for their own actions. Anne Lamott said it beautifully: "I did not know that help is the sunny side of control. But now I know that it is defeating and abusive to try and get people to do what I was sure would help them."

I want to be clear that I know now that the particular obligation that led me to falling asleep in the drive-through line *was self-imposed.* My mother had been battling (reoccurring) cancer for more than twelve years. I was a mother of three, back in school, and working part-time. Because I lived out of town from her and could not "help" my mother as I wanted, somewhere in this emotional rollercoaster ride, I decided I would spend one weekend a month driving to her home, helping with household chores, and making meals for her to heat up when she got off work.

I did not examine whether this was a good idea because I made it into an obligation. With some discernment, though, I asked myself why I was driving across two states to clean someone else's house (all weekend) and it began with the simple question, "Why did I start doing this caretaker action in the first place?" I journaled for a few days on this one question and boiled my thoughts down to one sentence: I wanted my mom to have a clean house to come home to when she didn't feel well (Read: I wish *I* had a clean house to come home to, so she must want one too). I thought this action would let her know I cared, I loved her, and I wasn't too far away to be on "Team Bobbi." She had an amazing group of people who were cheering her on through cancer survival and I wanted to be part of that team even when living over 600 miles away.

I need to explain something about my mother. She was my best friend. She was a best friend to many people. How so? Let's just say it was because of her chair. My mother owned a beauty salon. Her chair at the salon was where she was the best friend or therapist to half the women in our hometown. People came to her because she was good at styling Big Hair (Southern girls know what I mean). But she turned clients into friends because she could make them "feel pretty" when they looked in the mirror. That's what she told people she did for a living: she "made people feel pretty." Since momma had survived cancer herself, and she proved that we don't even need hair to feel pretty even when chemotherapy snatches it right off our heads. How? She spent years volunteering in hospitals teaching people how to wear scarves and wigs and sometimes how to stick rhinestones directly on a bald head and (still) look amazing.

Self-Control *is* Being Loving

Now I've told you the bigger story. I began to discern by asking myself an open-ended question: *Why I was cleaning her home?* Answer: *I wanted her to feel loved. I wanted to give her what I thought I would want if I was in her shoes.* Then the questions really started rolling: Is cleaning her house the only way I can do the things I intended? If I want her to feel loved, but was spending all my time cleaning—instead of hanging out with her—was that best use of my time? My resources? My offer of love?

Now that I had some insight I knew what to do next; I made the list of things that give me peace (You built that list of things that gives you a sense of peace in the Chapter 3 exercises). So now here's my second big confession for this chapter. One of my favorite things to do, that gives me a sense of peace, is watching house-makeover TV shows. I love those shows! One show that was popular back in the early 2000s gave me chills (or tears) every time I watched. The producers organized friends and a local volunteer group to fix up a house for a person who usually had been spending all their free time and resources helping others. That's when I got the idea—I would do a makeover for Momma! My strengths were organizing groups of people to accomplish a task, having fun, and stretching a dime as far as a dollar. I could do this! I had almost a whole month before I headed back home for that "outdated obligation." How would I find the resources to make this happen? I decided to pray and plan it out.

The Plan for Momma's Big Makeover

The plan looked like this. I asked: "What could be done if I had twenty-four hours and a few friends and family to help?" That narrowed the idea down to time (24 hours) and labor (how many people I could fit in her house), so I knew we could probably only do the most important things for her recovery: (1) paint her bedroom and the main living area a fresh and cheerful color; and (2) redo her bathroom so it became a space that felt calm in the midst of the trauma when puking her guts up from the chemo she received every month.

Then it got fun. I made a list of all the people who had ever said to me "let me know if there is anything I can do for your momma." Now was the time to call in those offers. I asked them all to consider helping with my plan by giving time, financial resources, materials (like paint brushes), or skills (like hanging wallpaper or cleaning). Oh, and they had to keep it a secret from Momma.

On the day of the great makeover, family members, clients, and friends showed up and chose a task they wanted to do, from a list of jobs needing done for this occasion. We had collected enough money to pay for professional painters. People brought cleaning supplies and clean linens, shower curtains and kitchen curtains, paper towels and wallpaper. The grandchildren were put in charge of cleaning all the windows inside and out (they found some pretty creative ways to do that task) and everyone worked *around* the painters and wallpaper hangers. It was a beautiful, eclectic dance. It was a surreal world of controlled chaos. Everything I had dreamed up and put on that prayer list happened that day.

Insight Does Not Always Bring a Disney Type of Ending

Now is this just another happily-ever-after story of what can happen if you listen to the fruit of the Spirit? No, not really, because Momma did not have long to enjoy her gift. She passed on within five months of the great makeover.

But! This was where not only *my* divine caregiver and human caretaker selves connected, I know that this connection happened for others that day as well. How? Because, on the day of her funeral, people were still talking about how much fun they had serving her during that great makeover. By looking at *why* I was doing *what* I was doing, from a bigger perspective, I had *allowed* more people in the picture to share their love for my momma. Not only those who came to help, but those she told while sitting in her chair—she spent weeks bragging about the tremendous difference it made to her that she came home each day to a space that was so obviously full of love from friends and family.

I have not planned such a big project ever again; frankly, I hope I never get the urge to do such a crazy stunt in the future. That said, I still drove to visit Momma each month, but instead of cleaning, Momma and I would do fun things together—we called it making memories. One night we met her sisters at the bingo hall. Another time we drank chocolate martinis and ate White Castle cheeseburgers for dinner, just because we could. Those are some of the best memories I have of being the out-of-town member of Team Bobbi. Those are the human-meets-the-divine times that I think of often when I am missing her now.

Suggested Exercises

Learn to start a sentence with the words "I need." The words *I need* can seem strange to people who are the helpers in our society. Often we are the ones who fall into the trap of codependent relationships. Being in a codependent relationship affects our ability to have healthy interactions with people because we desire approval from someone, which falsely builds in patterns of negative self-worth or an identity dependent on "fixing" someone else. This exercise teaches you to bust free of the shackles you wear as a caretaker who ignores your caregiver spirit.

Get a piece of paper and a timer. Set the timer for two minutes and write a list of your greatest weaknesses. Stop after two minutes. Then turn the paper over and set the timer for another two minutes. This time list your greatest strengths. Just keep writing until the timer goes off.

Now. Look at both sides of the paper. How are they different?

I suggest that the list of your weaknesses is longer than the list of your strengths. I also guess that on the strengths' side, you started a sentence or two with "I am good at," followed by a task that is all about serving other people or connecting with people by serving.

Knowing our weaknesses better than our strengths happens to many of the people I have asked to do this exercise.

1. Why do we have an easier time saying what we are weak in than admitting what we are strong in? Write this question in your journal and spend all the time you want discerning the answer.
2. Write one caretaker task you are doing for someone in your family. Ask yourself why you are doing this task and then figure out whether you should continue doing it or replace it with something else, maybe something that better suits the purpose of why you do it. (Trust me on this one: I am *not* asking you to plan a house makeover. I am simply asking you to pick one small thing that you already do that others may be waiting to help you with.) You might be surprised how good it will feel for them to have a place to show some love too. My grandchildren love to help me set the table and cook with me when they eat at my house. It takes longer to do these tasks with them helping me, but sure makes sweet memories for us all.

*** Remember: Sadly, there are studies showing family members are at the top of the list for abusing our aging population. If you see someone being struck, or starved, or laying in old feces, PLEASE ***don't wait***. Call 911 immediately! Then call together the family; many decisions need to be considered. Family will be needed to help on many levels. Call your clergy to help mediate the family if you can not get to a professional therapist.

Chapter 7

Non-judgmental Faith

"Faith is being sure of what you hope for and certain of what you do not see."
– Hebrews 11:1

"…preserve sound judgment and discernment, do not let them out of your sight; they will be life for you, an ornament to grace your neck."
– Proverbs 3:24

"Faith is never a matter of doctrine and principles. It is action. Faith in this way becomes a wager: faith is then not something we have, but something we do which is perhaps the best antidote possible to the despair and distrust that paralyze."
– Cynthia Bourgeault, Teilhard for Troubled Times

W hen Katie (age thirty-two) smiles, it makes people around her smile. She pulled back her long, straight, brown hair in a pretty ponytail holder which she kept pulling out and retightening again. She came to talk to me after recently moving in with her father, Mike. This arrangement began as a financial buffer. Katie had spent most of her career as an RN at a local hospital. She had decided to become a physician's assistant, after taking a nursing position in a pediatrician's office. A doctor she had come to admire suggested Katie consider getting a higher degree in medicine. After talking with friends and her father, she was ready to try.

The *best thing about living with her father* was that she felt she was starting to relate to her father as an adult, not just a dad who took care of her while she was growing up. Her mom had died two years before, but in her mom's last year of cancer Katie would spend many nights at her parents' home, helping with the complicated medical needs. She also came over for emotional support. Her mother loved French fries, so Katie would surprise her with different take-out versions. She loved those times when they would sit in bed, eat fries, and watch TV together. It was like having an adult slumber party with her mom.

Since Mike (age sixty-one) did not let Katie pay rent, she tried to think of other ways to contribute to the household. Pretty much the basic chores were organic enough to flow back and forth between the two of them. Katie had no problem cooking and doing the household chores because they were the things she would do if she were living alone anyway, and her dad was the same way.

Assumptions, Interpretations and Mind-Reading Skills

What she *wished she had known about before she moved back home* were the many uncomfortable assumptions that were made because she was the daughter and he was the father. Who would buy groceries? Who would pay for a meal if they go out to dinner? These became uncomfortable conversations for her, especially since her dad was generous and he always insisted on paying. These were becoming "a battle" that Katie felt she must always concede to, as the daughter. But being "the daughter" carried over into other issues. For instance, if she broke, borrowed or moved something in the home she felt like an eight-year-old again.

Once she borrowed her father's canoe, and while using it camping with friends, she lost one of the life jackets. "I told my dad I was really sorry and I would replace it the following week, but he gave me his I-am-so-disappointed-in-you dad look. I hate that look. It has begun setting me off, and I am doing things that are just not like me. It's been over a month and I still haven't replaced that life jacket. I just don't want to see the disappointed look he might give me when I hand it to him. I am getting that disappointed dad look too often. Even for simple mistakes like spilling coffee on the couch."

She continued: "I am beginning to be uncomfortable in my own home. I want to relax, maybe put out some of *my own thing*s in the living areas. I have all my stuff packed in boxes in the basement. Originally, I had planned to stay at home for the two years it will take to finish my degree. I just don't know if this is good for our relationship. He is the only parent I have left."

After bravely telling me her innermost concerns, Katie's beautiful smile tilted sideways on her lips, and it was no longer showing in her eyes. "It sounds so petty when I say it out loud, but how do I get my dad to treat me more like an adult instead of a child?"

Childhood habits can make independent core identities run amuck. Moving into an established home where a cohesive whole has assumed roles formed in the past can be tricky. Most of us have experienced how our (natural) identity as an adult in the outside world can often become colored a different shade, by the lens which our parents view us. How we *interpret* the ways our families "see us" are the background stories to most comedies written about going home for the holidays. Then again, some adult children (consciously or not) begin acting like children the moment they come in contact with a parent.

People Like Living with Family Members

In a nutshell, *how* we act like an "adult" in a family situation may depend upon how secure our core identities are to begin with. Being secure in who you are can allow you to see "the other" person in the room with less judgment (assumptions) and more faith (compassion) in who they are as independent, individual, beings. Good news—studies are showing up to 49 percent of adults surveyed who have moved (back) into their parents' homes believe that moving home has been very good for the relationship between them. Additionally, over 60 percent of the parents surveyed who say they have had an adult child move back home think it has been good for their relationship as well.

It has been said that intelligence is the ability to hold two opposing ideas in your mind at the same time and still be able to function. When we assume that our roles as children could transfer seamlessly into our new roles as adults, in our family of origin, we can get angry or frustrated, pushing us away from healthy functioning. Our actions (and reactions) have been infused with what we believed as children, but our time away from family is where we gain most of our individual adult habits and identities.

This experience of loving our parents (as an adult vs. as a child) has actions which hold a power over some large consequences. An example of how to break down this paradox is: Love is a noun (it shows person, place or thing) *but* loving is a verb (it shows action). Have you ever wondered how a person can say they are in love with you, but then are not acting loving toward you? Same thing for parents and adult children. They have to start looking at love from the lens of one adult to another adult. This lens calls for assumptions to be challenged with the actions found in Non-Judgmental Faith.

Katie and her father were having experiences/assumptions common to many of those who are in Generation X and Y and have boomeranged home. These people generally have graduated high school or college, and after leaving to live on their own, have returned to live with parents, thus the term boomerang. This has become more common in our society since the 1990s. These boomerangers are not moving home due to poor health as are the baby boomers. Millennial boomerangers, and those of Generation X and Y, are returning home due to economic downturns and marriages occurring later in life.

Studies of This Social Phenomena Agree in Several Areas

Many adults in their 20s and 30s are boomeranging back into their parents' homes due to debilitating student loan debt. Contributing to that debt was the economic instability of the Recession of 2008 which caused a decrease of funds being allocated by parents to help with higher education. This has resulted in Americans owing over $1.48 trillion in student loan debt that is spread out over about 44 million borrowers. The average class of 2016 college graduate has over $37,000 in direct loan debt. Also, the higher the degree, the larger the debt. So, if a person attempts to get a graduate degree, say a master's in science, their *average* loan debt will be closer to $50,440.

Within multi-generational families, studies are also showing we need to (re)learn how to communicate after being forced into these lifestyles. Some research is starting to surface, claiming that long-term relationships can be damaged when members of a multi-generational family are not able to learn to (re)negotiate, in ways they did not need to when the children where pre-adults. There are, therefore, many critics of this multi-generational living situation who "worry about the negative effect this trend has on the financial and social independence of the children." Others are claiming that the unrestrictive nature of living alone, or in a college dorm, makes it hard for people to readjust to shared living spaces with a parent. Others say that dating is being negatively affected by a stigma in our culture, claiming that an adult person who is not capable of independent living is too emotionally impaired to have a productive relationship.

As someone who has lived with a parent as a young adult, and as someone who has lived with adult children as the parent, I contend that multi-generational living can be really good for long-term relationships, both during—and after—these living arrangements are over. One way to make this all work is to be willing to learn how to communicate within a framework of non-judgmental faith.

Non-Judgmental Faith

The main English definition of the word *judgment* is "the ability to make considered decisions or come to sensible conclusions". The second definition is "a formal decision given by a court". In Greek the exact word *judge* only appears in the form of judgment where the broader root meaning is "to part" or "to sift," with the most common meaning being "to decide".

This word, in the original Hebrew, is used only in relation to a name for someone who "rules." But even the wisest of rulers would hesitate to judge people. King Solomon, proclaimed wisest of all kings, did not dare to assume his heart was understanding enough or discerning enough to judge others (1 Kings 3:9). Even more important to note that even Jesus claimed he "did not come to judge the world, but to save the world" (John 12:47). The only judge Jesus would acknowledge was the Creator (John 12:49).

Therefore, our definition of LIVING a Good Life with Non-Judgmental Faith is the ability to adjust negative assumptions of others toward a more complete confidence in people who are doing the best they can with what they have been given.

When using a more whole definition of non-judgemental faith, what could it mean to adjust negative assumptions? This brings me to my first of two thoughts on judgment:

1. We are amazingly blessed to be living in a society with free speech, yet we can often act as if judgment can also be freely passed onto others (with our words). Our unconsidered spoken words, or quickly given opinions, do not make sensible conclusions and yet we are okay with personally passing judgment on other people. To be more specific: name calling, "*she is so stupid;*" labeling, "*all young people today are so lazy;*" othering/prejudice, "*Those (insert nationality/ethnicity) are just not like us*;" lastly, and most common, is giving a "heated or emotionally laden opinion" on any issue we do not know much about. When we are honest with ourselves, most heated opinions are subjects we probably **could not** fill up a 3x5 index card with well-thought-out information or proven facts. Yet, we defend our limited knowledge often with name calling, labeling, othering or division tactics.

2. Being non-judgmental is when someone realizes and is consciously aware that they are not appointed to be a judge of the world or of other people. But even when we become conscious of our narrow version of judging, it is very hard to stop. It can challenge our belief systems and make us doubt we know what is right or wrong to do in many situations. We have been taught to think from only our own point of view. Non-judgement takes the more honest position that another version of a story could be just as good, and just as valid as your own. Or as my favorite rabbi says, "I do not have to be wrong for you to be right". While learning this perspective can be hard work,

it is also amazingly freeing. I will discuss how, after attempting to define the word Faith in this context.

Merriam-Webster defines *faith* very simply as "a complete trust of confidence in someone or something." What is interesting is that in the original Greek, the word used for faithfulness—as a fruit of the Spirit—means to "hold fast" or "steady." It also refers to one of the strongest personal characteristics of the Creator as being a covenant-maker. References to being a covenant-maker are first found in Hebrew scriptures where the Creator is referenced as being faithful to all Divine promises, *even when we don't stick to our side of the covenant.* This is one of the reasons that Judeo-Christian theology came up with the concept of an unconditionally Loving Creator. Having an unconditionally loving Creator can mean we don't have to be perfect to be loved.

Steadfast in Faith vs. the 'What If' Game

With a very small form of piety I have claimed that I was not God, but often my actions showed that I could quickly fall into passing (my own form of) judgment. I still find it very hard not to judge people who I feel wronged me personally in some way, shape or form. That means that I must often consider where, when, and how I fall into judging someone or something. The easiest way for me to start was by becoming mindful of when I became negative about *anything* that had to do with my view of other people. Mainly, I had to stop letting my negative opinions come out of my mouth. How? I began to give up using the words *always, never,* and *they,* and give thought to the concepts *good or bad, right or wrong, better or worse, us or them.* I had to start actions that assumed the best in and from people.

Assuming the best in people is really hard work. One reason for me, is that I quickly fall into playing the "what if" game. Here's how it's played: I come to the conviction that judging is not my job and I want to stop. Then the "what if" monster shows up and says, "So, *what if* someone is a murderer and they—" Wait. Nope. No, no, no. Sneaking in a "what if" question is nothing but a distraction to the point I am making. How does the concept of murder, which belongs in a courtroom, really have anything to do with me personally not passing judgment on someone with my mouth? My mouth is letting out what my heart is claiming that I know. I must remind myself: Is what another person is thinking, doing, choosing, or becoming something that I am allowed to pass judgment on? If not then when my opposing thoughts like the "what about a murderer, shouldn't we judge a murder?" jumps into the middle of my conviction with this type of far-flung possible scenarios I can choose the non-judgemental path. I contend that most "What ifs" are where our negative emotions run amuck. Therefore, I often have to remind myself that I have two choices when the "what ifs" show up.

The first and most natuarally occuring choice is where I could continue to think scary or negative thoughts. I get stuck and end up feeling a need to control a horrible *Lord of the Flies* type event that *could* happen in my life. I could let my unfounded emotions about how judging has a positive v.s. a detrimental place in our society distract me. I could even continue thinking the worst until I start to live unconsciously as the victim, judge, jury, and the executioner of a crime that *has not even been committed*.

Or, I could stop. Breathe. And refuse to play the game with the "what if" monster. Being non-judgmental, or seeing where our opinions are not the gold standard of measurement on *anything or anyone*, allows the pressure to be off of our thoughts. Holding steadfast to assuming the best in everyone empties us of guilt, shame, or a pain-filled ego by choosing not to pass judgment on ourselves or others. Did you see me

the misnomers in our "we were living alone together" statement. In our case, how a family *should act* brought forth opposing ideas in our minds and our actions.. We were wasting a lot of energy on being right (read: judgments) about what a good family looked like because we came from two good families that acted nothing alike. Therefore, healthy, productive, faithful functioning just could not happen. Thankfully, there was family counseling offered at the free clinic on campus. Okay, hold your hats, because this is where I could blame our mothers for our fight.

Blaming the mother makes everything easier, right? No. Not really. Our fights were not because we were raised by horrible people. They were *both* good, loving mothers. Yet, neither woman *showed love* like the other woman in concrete actions. One was a stay-at-home mother and one was a single mother that owned her own business. Being raised with two different views of what love looks like, and claiming we knew the right way to love made our everyday actions come into conflict often.

These opposite "opinions" (read: judgments) of what loving actions looked like were hard on our very limited amount of intelligence. The pain was so real I can still remember having these thoughts: *If I did not make breakfast for my husband did that mean I did not love him? If my husband expected me to make him breakfast every morning did he love the real me? If neither of us is eating in the morning then who makes breakfast for the baby before we both head off to school and work?* Thirty-four years later these thoughts (influenced by daily actions that defined what we thought was loving) seem silly, petty, and culturally laden with assumptions. Having two loving mothers set us up to have our first married fight because we judged their actions as being the loving way to be in a marriage. Our biggest most impassioned fight which made us consider divorce within three months of living on our own was over the critical issues surrounding which breakfast cereal was better: Post Raisin Bran or Crispy Wheats & Raisins. Or was it?

Remember, No One Can Read Minds

Assuming that we know what people are thinking because they give us "a look" is being judgmental. Katie assumed she knew how to interpret her father's thoughts about losing something based on past experiences of her eight-year-old self. Katie had to decide how to stop judging her father, and stop blaming him for her reactions. Katie began to see where she could start treating her father like an adult roommate instead of wasting time and energy wishing he treated her like one. What she had to gain was faith in her father. She began practicing empathy or to "walk in the other person's shoes." She then realized that *anyone* would be sad, if they had lost something they liked, right? Especially something that held sentimental value. Camping was what the *whole* family had done together over the years. Her father had his own backstory to that camping gear.

Katie was then able to consider her father was an adult with his own stories (and that he should not have to explain why he was disappointed). Her father was a good person. She began to restart and to rethink from that position whenever she began judging him when he gave her "that look." She was not eight years old. She was an adult, and she claimed it by not assuming she could read his mind any longer. She could be a grown up and still be his daughter, these roles were not mutually exclusive.

The same held true of my own story in the new role of being a wife and a mother. After living the first year of marriage in a house with roles *clearly defined* by childhood memories within my husband's parents' home, we now had to set up our own home. I had to become secure about my role and actions because at the beginning of our marriage our actions were framed very differently from the ones expected in our previous home. How? Let's boil down what was happening in the cereal war. My new husband's mother had made him breakfast every morning. The same role was expected of me when we lived in their home. When we moved into married student housing I said something like 'no' to making him breakfast anymore. I lovingly bought cereal and assumed he knew what that meant. So even though we were deeply in love, our judgments were preventing us from acting from a place of being loving. We were expecting undiscussed roles. We were assuming mind-reading skills that did not exist. Bottom line: We had to learn to consciously spend more time acting like adults in our own home instead of like children who wanted the other to approve or agree with us to get validation. It was hard, but the work paid off. And it is still paying off into many areas of our lives today.

Suggested Exercises

The following exercises are two I have been using for years to help me remember to live more faithfully, by remembering that others were also created in the image of our Loving Creator. They build on the previous exercises. First, we will remember a good or best thing about someone, and then we will follow through with actions that can make the relationship better, stronger, and healthier. These actions will be based on reflection within any of the fruit we have been given: Peace, patience, kindness, gentleness, goodness, and self-control.

1. "If you can't say something nice, don't say anything' at all."

Saying only nice or encouraging things about people sounds a bit too good to be true. What if I told you that medical science tells us that we are able to live longer, be happier, and feel more satisfied with our lives if we would change one small thing: Be compassionate.

As I have mentioned before, compassion is practicing empathy, but now we are going to begin thinking within a version of the golden rule. "Do unto others as you would want them to do unto you." We are going to explore this golden rule further in the next chapter, but for now let's do something measurable to get our heart, soul, and caring spirit facing in the right direction.

In your *LIVING* journal, start giving yourself a smiley face (a simple drawing or stickers if you want) in the upper right-hand corner each day you give *anyone* a sincere compliment. The goal here is to begin to think of others in a positive way. Give two people a compliment, give yourself two smiley faces. Sounds easy, right? When you are ready to do this, continue it for one week. If that sounds too easy, then take it to the next level.

Within one day, give everyone in your house a compliment. Just one, but *everyone, no exceptions, no excuses.* Then give yourself a smiley face (and a gold star).

When this becomes easy, think of five positive things about each person in your home, write them down on sticky notes, and attach them to the doors of their bedrooms. This is a very brave action, especially if you are still working through some hard feelings that are pushing you backwards into childish behaviors, instead of forwards into the adult actions. This public exposure of your renewed thoughts can be scary. *What if* you are rejected in some way? *What if* they never talk to you about the note you left on the door? *What if* they accuse you of something (in a passive aggressive reaction) in their own guilt about seeing your changing caregiver heart? Are those "what ifs" pushing to play? Can you say no to them and seek out what is good for your caregiver spirit instead? These suggestions are simply that, suggestions. If emotions around your home are too big for these small actions, please consider spending time with a trained professional. If you cannot afford one, seek out your pastor for direction and guidance in these matters.

When all those previous choices become more of a habit, then take it to the next level and reflect on the following: Do I generally watch what I say to people? Do people generally see me as being an encouraging person? If so, why? If not, then why not? Most importantly, now what?

2. Choose to be in positive spaces. Psychologists are saying that they can predict if a marriage will last, or not, by counting how many positive interactions we have (with our spouse) verses how many negative interactions we have. They are also claiming it takes five encouraging statements to remove the damaging effects of one negative statement. In the spirit of having faith or a complete trust of confidence in someone regardless of whether they return the sentiment, try the following *three tasks* for *the next three days in a row.*

   a. Smile more.

   b. Start writing down one event that you are grateful for each day before you go to sleep. The thing you are grateful for does not have to be a big thing—like world peace being discovered (even though that would be really really nice). It can be even the smallest event which had a positive impact on your heart, or mind, or strength that day.

   c. Choose to be in only positive spaces for three days. You will talk to positive people, say positive things, and read, listen to, or enjoy positive items on your list of "things to do that make me feel at peace" list from the exercise in Chapter 3. If you have a hard time finding or being in those spaces for whatever reason, this is a great reason to reflect with writing in your *LIVING* journal. Why is this exercise difficult for you to try or to do? Figure it out, then do it; three days is long enough for a resurrection to occur in your faith, just saying.

Something to consider when you are choosing to be in positive spaces:

My dearest friend is a social worker. She is one of my heroes of the faith, as her chosen profession is to help juvenile boys attempt to deal with some of the issues that have brought them one step away from being sent to prison. You would think that her job would keep her from being in a positive space for three days straight. Well, that is where you'd be mistaken. These boys may have such major issues that they have been institutionalized by the state at a "boys' home," but that space is transformed because of who my friend *IS*. She has been able to surround her staff and her boys with giving and positive experiences. I have watched her boys when they see her. Many faces light up when she walks by, as they feel she both loves and likes them.

I also have a new friend who, in the courtroom, defends women and children who have been abused. That type of court space is inherently sad and painful. She does not have the authority or the healing that is going to be needed to change all those wounded hearts. Yet, she does have the power to protect them from it happening again, which is a start on the long road to recovery. This friend knows that her professional calling is hard. I honor her courage to fight for the wounded among us. But she also knows she *must intentionally* use her weekends to be in positive spaces in order to keep up the good work she has been called for. She therefore intentionally sets up her weekends to be in positive interactions for her emotional and spiritual health.

Chapter 8

Guiding Joy

"Comparison is the thief of Joy."
– **Theodore Roosevelt**, US President and conservationist

"Do unto others as you would have them do unto you."
– **Golden Rule**, Matthew 7:12

"Discovering more joy does not save us from the inevitability of hardship and heartbreak. In fact, we may cry more easily, but we will laugh more easily too. Perhaps we are just more alive. Yet as we discover more joy, we can face suffering in a way that ennobles rather than embitters. We have hardship without becoming hard. We have heartbreaks without being broken."
– **Desmond Tutu**, South African cleric and theologian

Every year on November 16, I start getting some exciting emails reminding me that today is "Stephen's Day!" I have been receiving these messages, and the great news of how people are celebrating (all over the country) for over ten years now. Stephen's Day is similar to the concept of *passing it forward*. People either plan, or become consciously aware, of giving something to a stranger with the one caveat being that they do not expect anyone to know it was them, as it is done in honor of Stephan. It is gift giving in its purest form.

What makes Stephen's Day a bit different from the pay it forward movement is that it was started by some of my very close friends. Their son Stephen was a man who had spent a few years in the captivity of addictions. When he became free from those torturous, destructive demons he was amazingly good at seeing the hidden people in our society. Some might say he had developed his noble empathy because he once walked among them. Others might believe he became one of the (healed) wounded warriors who would spend his life helping others, those that he once was a part of. Stephen could get the downtrodden to *feel seen again* and thus worthy to be helped.

Stephen died in a car accident on November 16. People who knew him during the (too short) twenty-five years of his life knew about the hope he was giving to so many people. We knew he loved to help people, with even the basics, needed for survival on the mean streets of Atlanta. Just weeks before he died, he was in New Orleans rebuilding houses for Katrina victims. So, while recovery gave Stephen a larger purpose in his life, I am absolutely certain that Stephen had inherited his insightful talents for bringing joy to others from his parents.

Having 'Hardship without Becoming Hard'

I have known Stephen's parents for over 25 years. Even before Stephen (and his brothers) became such amazing servants, his parents were known as people who spent their lives serving the widows and orphans, as their own personal calling. Even now, when many of us are hitting the age where we should be taking it easy, if this couple gets wind of a person with a physical or mental illness needing something, they will find a way to meet that need. It could be something as simple as a ramp to help get a wheelchair user in and out of a home and they will show up with a team of grace-filled workers to measure, supply, and build that essential ramp, allowing a person who was once a shut-in have access to the beautiful world outside.

So, Stephen's Day has become more than just one day where a bunch of people get an email reminding us of the faith and love of this remarkable man (and his family). We are not just honoring one man, or one family, we are honoring all those who are in hardship as a way to keep even ourselves from becoming hard. We are simply putting the golden rule into practice, and the consequences are endless.

This is a truth that is both complicated and simple at the same time. Because by serving others, we are also serving ourselves. We are partnering with someone, even if it is with neighbors we do not know. One way this divine meeting of our caring selves happens is when we witness, while embodying the golden rule, the life-giving change that can affect both parties. My grandfather would say, it is like "sticking a thumb in the eye" of all the negative media whirlwind around us, day in and day out. It's so welcoming to see the moments that remind us that the vast majority of our world is full of caregivers, compassion seekers, and young people who want to honor the memory of those they love.

Our Caring Selves Connected Together
Guide Joy into our World

Being the people who are filling the role of caretakers, for our aging parents and financially struggling adult children, we are practicing the golden rule *daily.* Why do we forget that? Maybe, it is because we do these actions daily. Maybe it's because we don't consider taking care of family as heroic even though it can be so challenging. If we met someone whose *career* was to meet the needs of millions of Americans with neurodegenerative disorders and complications of aging, we would think, "Wow what a cool job, I wish I could do that."

Being caretakers for our families is a special role. We know, inherently, that *we too* are benefiting physically and mentally, living in a world that is consciously surrounding others with compassion. What if we don't acknowledge that? Several top universities have whole departments devoted to the study of compassion. Some of the work being done at Emory University leads me to think that the golden rule just may be hardwired into our brains and our hearts. These studies are proving that when students take a course in compassion training, their blood and saliva levels show they have lower stress hormones. Additionally, when participants undergo MRI measurements, the brain's pleasure systems show that they are firing even when *just thinking* about acts of compassion. Maybe this is what Desmond Tutu meant when he said, "...as we discover more Joy, we can face suffering in a way that ennobles rather than embitters."

At a recent conference at Stanford's Center for Compassion and Altruism Research it was also suggested that our brains may be hardwired to help others. There is activity triggered in the caudate nucleus and anterior cingulate parts of our brains, which are the portions which register and experience pleasure. Let's break that down into mainstream English for people like me. When I help someone, I may experience the same pleasure bursts in my brain as I do when eating a chocolate bar (but without the calories). What is being produced in our bodies, by helping others, is oxytocin, a hormone that floats throughout our bloodstream that may account for the feelings of warmth and connection we receive from warm smiles, loving gestures, and massages.

More research that suggests helping people is a biological need includes studies that measure how compassion affects us within our cardiovascular and respiratory systems. For example, when we feel threatened and get that fight or flight response, our heart rate elevates. Yet, when we are in caretaker/caregiver mode, our baseline heart rate goes down, which prepares us not to fight or flee but to "approach and soothe." The oxytocin flowing through our bloodstream then becomes self-perpetuating, and can motivate us to be compassionate again and again. Thus, this oxytocin response to wanting to alleviate suffering of others affects even our autonomic nervous systems. This may be why some of us label being in helping professions such as medicine, teaching, ministry, etc. a "calling".

Another reason that compassion may be boosting our well-being is it forces us to broaden our perspectives around us, and make us not think so often of ourselves. Research has often linked depression and anxiety to a state of being self-focused (with the exception of clinical depression). In 2015 the Bureau of Labor and Statistics reported at least 24.9% of Americans volunteered this shows that we innately choose to be outwardly focused. Clearly, recent scientific and governmental findings are challenging the discourse of our time, which contends that we as humans lean toward being selfish, brutish beings.

Neuroscience, evolutionary psychology, social science and many other academic disciplines are proving that *our own biology* actually is urging us to be compassionate. Meanwhile, the number of people taking care of our aging parents is rising into the millions, even while our national volunteer rates are showing that a quarter of our population is trying to alleviate suffering.

You may be wondering why I am talking about compassion when this chapter's title is Guiding Joy. Because even the Mayo Clinic is telling us that we have the choice to increase our levels of joy "as our thoughts and behaviors" can be changed through meditation, music, nature, letting things go, and gratefulness. Defining the fruit of joy as it is described in scriptures and in the twenty-first century gives us a better blueprint of how joy and compassion can be considered to be the same thing.

The English definition of joy is "a great feeling of pleasure and happiness or to rejoice." That doesn't tell us very much, so let's look in older languages. In Hebrew, the word for joy appears over 80 times and is found in 22 books of the Old Testament. It is used to describe mirth, gladness, pleasure and rejoice (or rejoicing) occurring in religious or festival atmospheres. In Greek, meanwhile, it appears over 50 times in 18 of the New Testament books, also describing cheerfulness and gladness, but it also means a calm delight or a gratefulness. When we look at the older definitions, we can see that joy is less about being "individually happy" and more about being "collectively thankful and appreciative."

That said, joy is listed as the third fruit of the Spirit—following peace, which, of course, I particularly like because in Proverbs we are told that "counselors of peace have joy" (12:20), and the larger meaning of the word in Hebrew is as a greeting used for thousands of years: "be well" or "thrive." Therefore, our larger definition of Guiding Joy when *LIVING* is a measurable wellness or a delight found in being thankful for our community and our family.

In *The Book of Joy*, recently written about the unprecedented meetings between Bishop Desmond Tutu and His Holiness the Dalai Lama, we see that compassion is a pillar that holds our joy in place. They met alone for five days to discuss one question: How do we find joy in the face of life's inevitable suffering? Both of these men are Nobel Peace Prize Laureates. They both have also spent most of their lives under politically oppressive violence and exile. Yet, they both also share the unique skills of practicing joy to "anchor their own emotional and spiritual lives."

"Discovering more joy does not save us from the inevitability of hardship and heartbreak," Tutu says. "In fact, we may cry more easily, but we will laugh more easily too. Perhaps we are just more alive." This strikes me as the very heart of why compassion is so necessary in our discussions of being caring selves.

The authors of *The Book of Joy* are caregivers and caretakers for entire nations, and they agree that the development or the building of empathy will not only change us individually, but also help prevent us from "building walls around ourselves," allowing us to remain joyful because we are not isolated and alone in our hardships. "We [can] have hardship without becoming hard. We [can] have heartbreaks without being broken."

The Golden Rule

Personally, I have been told there is no better way to display empathy and compassion than to live out the golden rule. My favorite faith-saving author, Karen Armstrong, claims that compassion is how we find ourselves "tuned into" our Creator's frequency. As one of the founders of Charter for Compassion, she tells a wonderful story of the Rabbi Hillel explaining a Jewish truth to a skeptical seeker. A man approached Hillel and claimed he would convert to Judaism if Hillel could recite the whole Torah standing on one foot. Hillel shifted to his right foot and said, "The whole sum of the Torah is to love your neighbor as yourself." He then stood back on both feet and said, "Now go, do likewise."

I have already told you the story of how seeing my need for better self care was shown to me after a tipping point that led me to sleep in a parking lot. After taking care of myself with a nap I was led to a larger truth by understanding a more personal role that the fruit of the Spirit has in my life.

Then I told you another story: How being conscious of connecting my caring selves together helped me to dream about the concept of Momma's Great Makeover. And also of being more about making memories than about cleaning the house. How much better I felt with my choices to be spending fun time together instead of completing every to-do list I could write.

I am now at the point in the story that I don't want to share. Which might be why I must. Even though I was now better at self care, less tired, and enjoying time with momma and my adult children more than I had in years, I was still *extremely sad*.

Why? How could that be? I am not suppose to be sad if I am a Christian, right? That must mean I am not confessing or repenting or something, right? *What if* this whole theory of practical theology and being promised fruits of the Spirit in real, life-giving, tangible ways was just hooey-phooey? *What if* all that Bible thumping malarky was not real, but just another tent show to fool the masses? Are you hearing my anger? Are you noticing the "what if" monsters that were grabbing me? I did not think I was being allowed to claim that I had the fruit of joy because I was still sad many days. I was ready to give up.

It took a while, but I finally decided to challenge my "what if" monster with a much deeper dive into why I was sitting at a pool of healing—but was I afraid to go in (John 5:1-8). Were these what if's just all the silly ramblings of a woman pastor? It was time to prove myself wrong. Time to figure out why there did not seem to be the fruit of joy in my daily life. I said "poo-poo on you" to the "what if" monsters—and a bit down in a stronger language by claiming (Bull-&*$%%!) to the horrible dogmas I still needed to shed—and dove deep into reflective scripture writing while focusing on what being a compassionate person could look like in ancient texts.

How? I began my new story by using the four questions that are given to us by a practical theologian named Richard Osmer. He teaches these four questions to graduate-level seminary students, but they really are not that hard (or I wouldn't not be using them as often as I do).

Using Practical Theology as a Way
to Think Inside of Scripture

Using Osmer's four questions helped me to understand how to make ancient text and even poetry relevant to me. Those questions are:

1. What is going on here?
2. Why is this going on?
3. What ought to be going on (or what do I need)?
4. How might I respond?

For the following example, I will put my caring selves in the role of the Roman Centurion (Matt. 8:5-12). This allows me to look safely "sideways" at the following text instead of head on, which can scare my shy caregiver self. It is a free-flowing exercise. It has no limits or boundaries. No right or wrong. It is simply being willing to place yourself inside of the text and write about the possibilities that come to mind. This is one way of practicing spiritual journaling or writing from the heart.

I began by reading quietly Matt. 8:1-12. Then I slowly wrote the text I just read. Writing forces me to slow things down and pay closer attention in order to engage. I look for the patterns of love, caring and useful actions within the texts.

1. What is going on?
Matt. 8:1-12.

As Jesus entered the village of Capernaum, a Roman captain came up in a panic and said, "Master, my servant is sick. He can't walk. He is in terrible pain."

Jesus said, "I'll come and heal him."

"No," said the captain. "I don't want to put you to all that trouble. Just give the order and my servant will be fine."

The word Capernaum jumped out at me as I wrote this scripture. Maybe because it is a space I know absolutely nothing about. Jesus was said to have "entered there" so I want to know where. I Googled "Capernaum" and found that this is the possible village of Peter, James and John. Which might explain how a Roman soldier (non-Jew) would know about Jesus performing miracles to begin with. This town or village is located directly on the Sea of Galilee where Jesus did a large part of his teaching.

"What is going on" then is a non-Jew in high authority has someone he cares about in need of healing. He is not afraid of his reputation and he believes (or has faith) that Jesus does not have to be physically present to heal his loved one.

2. Why is this going on?

Okay, this one is harder since I don't have much of a backstory in this text. So I will look at the language recorded in this text. Can the language/ words of the Centurion give me any Aha! moments?

The Centurion says: "He is in pain. He cannot walk." (8:2)

Nothing feels more distressing than seeing someone I care about in pain. When I see my mother in pain from her cancer, my first emotions are to feel helpless and scared. Not unlike the centurion, I want to do something to take away the pain. What can I do? I can talk to the doctor, I can make sure she has her medicine refilled and ready to be taken.

But I do not have access to walk up to Jesus and expect immediate relief for my mother's pain. That makes me sad, and I wonder why prayer won't work for this if Jesus doesn't have to be in the room. So this touches a core value about prayer in my faith tradition. Maybe I need to explore this further, later. I make a note of it and move on since I can nott really get what is going on yet in this context.

3. What ought to be going on (otherwise known as what do I need)?

My first thought was that I need my mother to get better, to stop hurting. Since I know my first thoughts usually come loudest from my caretaker self, I need to spend some time thinking about what my caregiver self wants/ needs in this situation. Why was I rambling on about emotions of fear and worry based on seeing my mother's pain? What was the reason? Had I been busy like I was before when I was always cleaning and had I just changed the busy cleaning into another form of busy under the premise of having fun instead? Hmmm, maybe. But this doesnt bring me an Aha…so keep going. Keep asking questions.

What if I just sat with Mom and allowed myself to be present in her pain? What would happen if I just sat down next to Momma and tried to notice the promised fruit of peace, love, patience, kindness, gentleness and self-control in the moment?

4. How might I respond?

If the centurion was able to ignore who he was (a non-Jewish soldier with a lot to lose by asking for healing) could I ignore that I am my mother's daughter? No, that's not what it's about. Why do I hate to see her in pain? Because that may mean she is closer to leaving me. I don't want her to leave. Aha… right there. Am I willing to not be worried? Doesn't worrying just make HER pain all about me? Can I sit with all my promised fruit and remember I am whole and filled and it is going to be okay for her and for me? This is what I will try the next time we are together.

My response next time we are together will be to try the following: I will sit with her and not make her pain about me. I am now willing to listen to what I am afraid of of hearing.

The exercise above is a sample of how I use Osmer's four questions to make myself ask the bigger questions. Some call this reflective journaling. Some even call it discernment. When I first started using these questions of practical theology in my life, I would write pages and pages of free-flowing thoughts. Nothing was held back. Journaling gave me a safe space to say everything I would not and could not say out loud.

Next I would read pages and try to narrow down my rambling to short or one-sentence answers. Often I couldn't. When that would happen I would have to walk away and come back to it the next day, or the next day. I would not stop until I could discern a simple or small need my caregiver self could identify and fill. I had to be patient in order to discern what direction I needed to try. The bigger the emotions the longer it would take me.

This is what I have to say about the time it took for me to discover the hidden joy I found in this exercise. When I sat with my mother, as I had planned from listening to my caring selves, the following happened:

She told me about memories and life events—with no agenda, no sorrow, only connection between a mother and a daughter. We laughed. We cried. We both napped a little in between. Later when I reflected on why I had not been spending time just sitting with her when she was in pain, I realized, that I knew her pain meant she was starting to leave. The pain meant the medication was no longer working. She was leaving and I did not want her to go, so I kept busy to distract me from *my* pain. I was losing her. I could take care of her no longer. That was when I could allow myself to be sad. I needed to be sad. I was losing my mother. It was time for self care. It was okay to be sad and fall into the compassionate joy with my community that was both human and divine.

It was time for my caring selves to work together, allowing me to feel the compassion needed to boost my well-being. The fruits were ripe to feed my spirit and I, like the centurion, was now the daughter who was ready to be faithful.

Accepting her death was forcing me to broaden my perspectives. And I was sad, and that was okay. This was no longer just about me because it was always bigger than that.

So I stopped "doing for" and started "just being" with momma from that point on. And I was sad, and it was finally okay to be sad.

And then Jesus said to the centurion (and the daughter): "Go! Let it be done just as you believed it would." And his servant was healed at that moment (8:13). And my mother touched the cloak of Christ and was healed in her own moment. I believed. She felt no more pain. She was called home—to be back with her own mother, and all our mothers before us who are walking with Eve in that beautiful garden with an eternal refreshing Spirit; our ruah.

And I was very sad and it was okay, I could be sad and joyful at the same time.

Suggested Exercises

Try your own version of reflective journaling using Osmer's four questions within Psalm 139. This is one of the first ancient texts I used when learning to reflect in scriptures. Working in reflection in the psalms usually gives sweet, soft, cool reflections from the edge of living water. If you want to ease into this idea a bit later try the first exercise below, instead.

1. This exercise is to help us remind our caring selves that we are all "beautifully and wonderfully made." Read and then slowly write the Love is… scriptures given in 1st Corinthians 13:4–8. After you write it all, go back and ask yourself, how may I learn to accept my gifts within that scripture? For example, "Love is kind: I am kind when I play cards with my mother, even though I want to watch TV," or "Love keeps no record of wrongs: My grandmother makes me feel like I can do no wrong and that is

a special skill; I hope I will be able to imitate her with my own grandchildren."

When you have listed all of them, put this in an envelope and write your address on it and mail it. You may find that you have more examples to add, *after* you receive this list back in the mail.

2. Write another letter to yourself using the following open-ended questions:
   a. What fruit do I hope to see growth in this year and why?
   b. When I spend time thinking about the fruit of love, I believe...
   c. When I reflect on what joy looks, I wonder...

Chapter 9

Living a Good Life

"… Then I grasped the meaning of the greatest secret that poetry and human thought and belief have to impart: The salvation of man is through love and in love. Now I understood how a man who has nothing left in this world may still know bliss."
— **Viktor Frankl**, Austrian neurologist and Holocaust survivor

"Until we know our hidden wholeness we will live in a world of dualisms, of forced but false choices between being and doing things that result in action that is mere frenzy, or in contemplation that is mere escape."
— **Parker Palmer**, Author and activist

"Religion says: God will love us if we change. The Gospel says: God's love changes us. Preach the Gospel at all times and when necessary use words."

— **St. Francis of Assisi**, Patron saint of animals

We have all heard of living the good life. One of my favorite T-shirts reads "Life is good" and it is made by an apparel company that is making clothing with optimistic slogans that are trademarked and sold in over 4,500 stores across the United States. The concept of "a good life" is so deeply ingrained in our culture that people are able to start companies just from printing the idea on shirts and accessories. But what is a good life? Is a good life something we can buy? Is it even a real thing? And if it is real, then can it be a space of endless possibilities or is it limited by something?

Whenever I have asked people the question: Could you please describe for me, in one sentence, "What is a good life?" most people will start off by saying, "Wow, that is a hard question," or "I have never thought about that before". What surprises me the most about the responses is that, even though I asked people between the ages of twenty-four and eighty-seven, they all gave a common answer. They all seem to believe that a good life is being in supportive relationships or being loved.

"A good life is about being happy because no matter how badly you mess up there are people who love you anyway."

"A good life is the ability to live free. And having people in my life to remind me that I am free when I forget."

"When you can live daily in a loving relationship with somebody."

"A good life has meaning while it is lived."

"A good life is having enormous blessings even when living in a fractured family."

We are not the first society to want a good life, even though we have definitely done a great job of promoting it through films, TV series, literature, songs and even ethics' classes. "The good life" is actually a philosophical term originally associated with the philosopher Aristotle.

Aristotle, like many of the great philosophers, loved to argue a point of logic. Philosophical arguments give me horrible flashbacks to debate classes, so I am going to shorten Aristotle's version a bit. His version of living a good life begins with a simple consideration of *ends* and *means*. Suppose I want to buy a T-shirt that reads "Life is good." That is the *ends*. I can earn the money, borrow the money, or even steal the money to purchase the shirt; that is the *means*. But, if we stop our definition of a good life right there, we are stuck in an economically driven and very narrow view of life. This is the view economists and commercial media push us to use in our culture. This is where the concept of a zero sum game steps in our path.

A zero sum game is where we have wants or needs (ends) and we have a limited amount of resources (means) therefore someone (probably us) *is not* going to get what they need because there is only so much to go around. Yet, Aristotle's concept of a good life was *also* about the unlimited "goods of the soul." He called these unlimited goods of the soul excellence. He then concluded that a good life is about living "excellence" found within the developing goods of the soul. Hmmm. Sounds very similar to what the apostle Paul was suggesting four hundred years later to the Galatians' churches.

When I ask people in the twenty-first century to describe a good life, even if they mention owning possessions, they also always include people they would want to share them with. The fuller and more whole definition of Aristotle's logic includes his theory that even if we were able to have everything we physically needed and wanted (health, pleasure, food, shelter, sleep, etc.) we *cannot* have more "goods of the soul" than we need. They will always need to be increased (unlimited knowledge, love, friendship, self-esteem, etc.). So it seems that throughout the ages we can all agree that *LIVING* a good life happens in a space of endless possibilities, personal growth, and rewarding relationships.

For the past seven chapters, I have given you a few open-ended questions for exploring individual paths to a good life. We will now learn how to ask our own open-ended questions. So when you finish this book, you can continue asking questions to bring comforting dialogue between your caretaker and caregiver selves. You will then also have a constantly updated map allowing powerful ways to rethink and rewrite your everyday narratives with excellence and holiness.

This chapter will be a place to find courage to challenge some of our core beliefs. We may even find a space to regain sight of the endless possibilities—in our absolute right to always be a work in progress.

A Work in Progress

Many people know instinctively how to comfort a child or a best friend. Yet, many of us do *not* know how to comfort ourselves. How is it we are sensitive to the suffering of others, but not to our own suffering? I suggest that we have spent so many years attempting to look acceptable, working hard to prove we are valuable, or taking care of everyone so that they will like us, that we do not see the pain our automatic responses are causing. We have forgotten our own need to be comforted and have stopped being loving to ourselves. Maybe because we are not loving ourselves we need to deaden the pain, so it is natural to turn to drugs or alcohol (or any addiction). Maybe because we are not loving ourselves we assume a false responsibility for others' happiness and wholeness. We live through making others being made happy and it is like using them to make us feel happy. We are using their happiness to fill up our own holes of unhappiness.

Learning to truly love ourselves can begin to remove the whys and hows and zero sum games we childishly or romantically play by living as though we have any control over how others act or feel. We forget to ask the very basic question of "Why do we want to make others happy?" Wanting to love others or make them happy is not a bad thing, is it? No. Loving actions are never bad. So what is the problem? Loving ourselves first allows us to remember it is not our responsibility, our purpose, or our right to make others feel or act a certain way in which we think, believe, or assume is right. Insisting that others feel, act, or behave in a way we want them to is actually unloving.

You may be reading this and thinking that loving ourselves just borders on heresy. Come on, preacher-lady, weren't you schooled on that by the Bible? Isn't it better to "give than receive," and to "take up our cross"? Don't you have any fear that loving ourselves can be arrogant or narcissistic, and even un-Christ like? A "good" person is not selfish like that, right? To the person questioning the paradox I am presenting when I say "you must love yourself first"—yes, it is more blessed to give than receive. Yes, it is important to learn to take up your cross in a real way instead of just a metaphor. And yes, I am in constant fear (read: high alert, not paralyzed with worry) that I could fall into selfish behaviors if I put myself first.

So, here's to living a good life within spiritual paradoxes: We are also told in sacred text, we must be willing to "Love our neighbors *as ourselves.*" From Genesis to Revelations, loving ourselves is claimed to be second in importance only to loving our God with our heart, soul, mind and strength (Mark 12:31). We are also told that love is greater than any spiritual gift (1 Cor. 13:1-3) and also that love is defined by actions (1 Cor. 13:4-7), not simply emotions. Therefore, love is being patient and kind *to ourselves.* Love is not being arrogant, rude, self seeking, or angry *with ourselves.* Love will not keep records of wrongs or rejoice in mistakes *we make ourselves.* Love covers a multitude of our own sins and rejoices in the truth. Why would it be so important to love ourselves? What if it is so that we can know how to love our neighbors without expecting anything in return? What if it is important to love ourselves only second to God so that we can see who are neighbors are? (1 Cor. 13:1-12)

If we ignore or dismiss loving ourselves with culturally misdefined concepts or false humility, then the love we are giving others offers a limited view of what is divine about love. If we hold to the teachings that our Creator God *is* Love, then refusing to love ourselves is dismissing what is divine in us. Taking a favorite sentiment by Maya Angelou, from the perspective of loving myself first, challenges my actions in daily life: "I've learned that people will forget what you said, people will forget what you did, but people will never forget how you made them feel." How can we give divine love if we do not accept it in ourselves?

I suggest we may not be loving to ourselves, not only because we have been taught culturally not to, but also because we are fearful of allowing ourselves to make mistakes or to be a work in progress. One reason is that life is not always good. Hard and bad things we have no control over have happened to us (divorce, abandonment, selfish or distant parents, job loss, dreams dismissed, abuse, etc.) and so we just move on in life by protecting our inner selves from our outer worlds. We live afraid of what is lurking deep within us so we organize our lives in ways that ensure nothing triggers the emotions we have worked years to control. This is why therapists are taught to create safe open spaces for dialogue. This is why we need to learn how to create our own safe spaces to have open and honest dialogue with caring for ourselves.

Open dialogue with ourselves can help us understand that having a fixed or protective mindset makes it too hard accept self-love. Protective unchanging mindset often cannot deal with the prospect of being a failure or failing. But when we can begin to be more loving to ourselves by asking open-ended questions, we can push past the thoughts of "things will always be hard" or "it is too painful to hope and be disappointed again." We can see our caring selves as a work in progress. We become capable of tremendous courage and never want to give up our right to be wrong. Making a mistake is okay. We have already been forgiven. That's what love does. Love gives and asks nothing in return.

Learning to ask open-ended questions

Learning to ask open-ended questions for self-reflection and for building rewarding relationships, with respectful dialogue, can show us the beauty hidden inside of people and ourselves. Why are open-ended questions better for reflection and dialogue? The frame from which they are hung tells a person you value their opinions, thoughts, ideas, feelings, etc. That they matter. You're asking because they matter.

Open-ended questions show people you are asking for their contribution and their information as a way to expand your own information and your own thoughts. Just by coming up with questions can make people think in ways that show we are intent on positive interactions. Let's start with some open-ended questions that were common for my husband and I to have around our family dinner table as our children grew up.

What is something new that you learned today or this week?

Did something or someone make you laugh this week?

What is the most challenging thing about the work at school? or at work?

For just plain fun ask these:

If you could only be allowed to eat one vegetable for the rest of your life, what would it be?

What is your favorite vacation, season, book, movie, or childhood memory?

What is the nicest thing a friend has ever done for you?

Maybe you noticed that the above questions are framed in a positive light but are still open to honest and deep responses. Negative questions bring negative feelings into the conversation. An open-ended question cannot be answered with a one-word response (yes, no, fine, okay, maybe, etc.).

Open-ended questions often begin with:

What

How

Who

Where

When

Words *not* to use in the beginning of a question:

Do you

Did you

Will you

Have you

Why don't you

Saying a sentence with the word "you" stops communication. It is a way to define the other person's actions or core identity, often forcing them to make an excuse or to defend an action or a core belief about themselves. Saying "you" in question form can hurt us. It makes us feel labeled or defined or dismissed. For example: I recently saw a small boy bump into one of those yellow cones that read "wet floor." He kicked that thing clear across the room. It was an accident. It was just a mistake—no puppies were killed, no one was damaged in any way. His mother scolded him in the form of a question. "Didn't you see that?" She then told him to "go get it and put it back." His mistake was made into a real source of shame—by a question. That was not an open-ended question.

Looking at open-ended questions with the *LIVING* model within our gifts will give you some examples to work with for your own open-ended questions. I suggest you read all six questions within the model. Then, if you choose to go back and answer any of them, I suggest you start with the one that "spoke to your heart." What does that mean? You will know when it happens—and it will happen.

L—Loving Your Peace. These are the life-giving actions of embracing a wholeness of our mind, body, and spirit. *What do I believe about being worthy to be loved by an unconditionally loving Creator?*

I—Integrity of Goodness. This is the ability to encourage with honesty that avoids all forms of harshness or cruelty by holding others in high esteem. *How can I see being loving to myself as a holy idea instead of just another rule or a law to follow?*

V—Valuing Patience. Having a high opinion of or respecting someone by yielding to the benefits of hope despite their actions is valuing patience. *Where do I need to grow in valuing others and how will this help me be patient?*

I—Insightful Self-Control. This is the ability to discern when our impulses, desires, or emotions should be tempered by considering that people are made in the image of a Divine Creator. *When or where have I seen that other people are created in the image of a Divine Creator, and how does this make me feel safe?*

N—Non-Judgmental Faith. The ability of non-judgemental faith allows us to adjust negative assumptions of others toward a more complete confidence believing people are doing the best they can with what they have been given. *What does or did feel like when someone I love or admire believes the best in me?*

G—Guiding Joy. This is a measurable wellness or a delight found in being thankful for our community and our family. *When I was a child, the person I loved being with the most was _____ because _____. (Example: When I was a child, the person I loved being with the most was my grandmother because she would tell me stories about...)*

As I mentioned before, if you choose to go back and answer any of the above questions right now, I suggest you start with the one that spoke to your heart. I promised you would know what "spoke to your heart" would mean when it happens. If you felt nothing, don't be discouraged;

that is exactly where you are supposed to be to learn what this means. I suggest you make a plan to spend a couple of hours (preferably outside) all by yourself to listen to your loving—never keeping record of a wrong soul, gently calling to your human self while answering all the above questions at one time.

Suggested Exercises

All previous exercises in *Living with Momma* have been as an offer of safe spaces for our souls to emerge within the context of our family stories. I have seen the following exercise used by social workers, ministers, and healthcare workers as a way to introduce self-care through healing and acceptance. We will look at a larger view of our (family) history and ask how it has defined our own stories. This exercise will use a genogram as a way to help us learn by uncovering some of the history that creates healthy and not-so healthy patterns in our families.

Simply put, a genogram is a chart that allows us to see patterns within a family system. We will then use this personalized chart to help us (re)write our family stories; or as Kierkegaard said it best, "Life can only be understood backwards; but it must be lived forwards." I gave you my own personal example of using a genogram to (re)write "being born into a family" in the closing paragraphs found in the introduction of this book. I took my genogram and reflected on the blessings *and* the wounds that needed to be seen through the eyes of an adult instead of my childhood. This is where I found my view of a good life.

1. Get a blank piece of paper, a ruler, and a pencil (preferably not a pen).

Set a timer for one hour. (I will explain why this is important later.) Begin the following:

- Draw a circle about the size of the palm of your hand right in the middle of the page.
- Write your full name, date of birth, present age, current or last occupation in that middle circle.
- On the right side of that (middle) circle draw another, smaller circle and then draw a line from that circle to your circle. Inside of that circle place the full name of your biological father. If you have a step-father or an adoptive father place another circle alongside of your biological father's circle and another line to your circle. Inside of each father circle, also place (like your own) his date of birth, present age, occupation. If this person is deceased, then lovingly place an X across his circle after you fill it in. If you do not know the exact dates (or exact information) of anything we are doing, that is okay; estimates will do just fine.
- On the left side of your circle do the same thing as you did on the right side but for your mother's information. Same as before, add any step- or adoptive mothers you have in your life and her birth date, present age, and occupation.
- In the space at the top of the page, do the same circle exercise with any children you have. Make sure you add those that are biological, adopted, and step-children.
- In the space at the bottom of the page, do the same circle exercise with any siblings you have had.
- Now it gets a bit wonky, but a lot more fun. Draw other circles that give the names and information of each of your parents' parents. Many of us in the sandwich generation are in our 50s and we knew our grandparents (so we might even have or at least been given firsthand knowledge of our great-grandparents). My own grandchildren are blessed to have two sets of great-grandparents (on my side of the family) to interact with.

If you really get into this kind of thing, add some aunts/uncles to this chart. You probably will not know their dates of birth, but may be able to approximate them based on your parents' ages, and you may also know their professions. Add these, as they can show a few more patterns in your family (behavior) systems.

Just remember you are not finished yet and you *only* have one hour. If you want to go further and do the whole Ancestry.com thing, good for you. I have fallen into that abyss myself at times. But researching your ancestry is *not* this exercise. When we get too far into other details we will never get to the real purpose of this exercise.

- Go back and add the following information (in capital letters) when you have finished adding all the people you can recall to your chart.
  - ❖ Did any of them fight in a war? Mark with a *F* on the top of the circle with their name.
  - ❖ Did any of them suffer the loss of a child? Put an *S* on the top of the circle with their name.
  - ❖ Did any have a college degree? Mark with a *C*. (If a person is beginning to have more than one letter, then just start going around the outside of the circle with all the letters surrounding their names).
  - ❖ Did anyone get fired or lose a business during economic downturns? Mark these with a *B* (as above).
  - ❖ Did any live through the Great Depression or the Dust Bowl (as in, lived between 1929–1939)? Mark with a *G*.
  - ❖ Are any of them first- or second-generation immigrants? Mark these with an *I*.
  - ❖ Were any of them widowed or widowers? Mark these with a *W*.
  - ❖ Were any of them divorced? Mark these with a *D*.

Hopefully you were able to finish your genogram within one hour.

If you are like me, at some point you will see many of the people will have several letters around their circles. As the lines connecting the circles will show you, every one of these people have or will have touched you, in one way or another. What I want you to consider is how most of them have survived (and even thrived) through some of the most hard- or grief-stricken times in life.

Take a minute and look at your genogram for patterns of survival.

- What comes to mind for you?
- Is this thought one of mindful character, heartfelt gratitude, and fruitful promises?
- What have you never considered before you saw this chart of your family in its entirety?
- How has being born into this family shaped your mindset to be responsible and motivated to make a difference in this world?
- What are you proud of?

I am not asking you to label any family member, mainly because it can lead to a judgmental spirit, and because as Kierkegaard also says, "Once you label me you negate me," but attempt to look lovingly at yourself and ask, "What patterns do I want to consciously hope *not* to repeat in my own life story?

Lastly, ask yourself, what does *LIVING* the good life mean to you now as you (re)write your family stories from the view of virtues, positive character traits, or fruit of the Spirit as your guide?

Chapter 10

Conclusion: The paradox of being human and being created in the image of God

"Despite how open, peaceful and loving you attempt to be, people can only meet you as deeply as they've met themselves."
– Anonymous

T he idea of people *LIVING* in spaces of peace, patience, kindness, goodness, gentleness and self-control may sound like a form of heaven on earth. Ideally, this book has given you a few ways to view this utopia within your own life by prompting movement from reflection to action. Some people will use the exercises and open-ended questions for transformative personal dialogue. Some will use the statistics and historical data for personal decisions to make changes from a more collective point of view. My hope is that this book offers countless possible insights from the many people who have found common ground in their good lives with family members.

Looking at our lives from a vista of positive change creates opportunity for us and those we come in contact with. The world is becoming a smaller place. People who once lived in far-flung places are growing more entwined with technology, immigration, and global trade. What is happening in one country impacts people in others, as shown even in the recent financial hardships that our families are facing in a twenty-first century global economy. A perfect paradox is found when as our world shrinks with global interactions our world view becomes larger with each connection we make.

This book then was birthed while I was in a personal quest to find a good life in this paradox of a shrinking and expanding world. I started this daunting task of listening to "my calling" to write this book a number of years ago. As one who has admitted to often seeking truths in paradox, this calling came when I had left the church and then enrolled in graduate studies at Columbia Theological Seminary. I was in a spiritual desert. I just did not know what a Universally Loving Creator looked like anymore. My view of any god had become small, old, and legalistic. Becoming a theologian gave me the keys out of the prison of laws and doctrines written by men who (unknowingly or not) insisted that I did not really matter that much. I was a descendent of Eve. Being born a woman had made me somehow culpable or the author of disobedience in the garden of Eden and someone who was really only created because Adam should not be alone. To that false doctrine and confining traditions I can now claim my Berean truths; Being in relationship with the Creator has nothing to do with rules, measurements or vain human wisdom (Mark 7:7; Matt 15:9; Col.2:22; Isaiah 29:13).

I held tightly to the keys seminary gave me and used them to open my own prison doors. I walked out into the light of a beautiful world given to us all by an Unconditionally Loving Creator. This book came about as a result of promises I gave my soul self. I would constantly be looking for safe places to be open and honest with self-reflection. I would find a tribe of people who refuse to live in the shadows cast by fear and would again enjoy exploring life as a child of the life-giving Creator God. And last, but not least, I would remember that I need to *look up* to pick fruit from trees before I can enjoy eating all the gifts hanging in wait.

It took years of sorting through churches and my own emotions of being a family caregiver/caretaker before I could tackle the binders and drawers full of social science information on American families I had collected over the years. That is when three different directions in writing began to come into shape. These directions became the three different perspectives I have written this book from: those being the perspectives of being an *insider,* being an *outsider*, and what anthropologists call being "a *connected critic*." You may have found yourself in all three perspectives as you read this book.

The Insider, the Outsider, and the Critic

When I took the paths of being an *insider* into writing *Living with Momma*, I came with a bias of two distinctly different life perspectives. First, I was raised within a home where the adults outnumbered the children. My parents and I lived, off and on, with my grandparents until I was approximately ten years old. My fondest childhood memories are based around a grandmother who made sure there were always Hershey's Bars in the freezer and a grandfather who loved to take me fishing for bluegill that we would later fry up in a big cast iron skillet.

Second, I also have been the parent who offered a home to my own adult children, when different life situations made it so that they needed a helping hand. I am now the grandmother who spends time spinning yarns, climbing trees, and talking to flower fairies with three of the most amazingly curious people ever placed in this world.

When I came to this book as an *outsider*, I was a pastor who offered counsel on this topic. I was given intimate, unguarded conversations with people who were living in close quarters with family. Most importantly, I was invited into their homes and blessed to observe and interact within their family settings. It was in those private spaces I attempted to glean awareness, and understand some of the nuances or gaps that an interview alone could not fill. This made me take time to ponder some reasons our present society does not look well on our renewal of extended family living together and created the *LIVING* concept as a way to push back against this misconception of family. I hope I gave voice to those who were actually enjoying these multi-generational homes. I loved every minute and every meal shared with these soul-seeking travelers.

And lastly, when writing this book as a *connected critic* (from the point of view of being a social scientist) before each interview I explained why I was asking the questions I did, and how the information might be used. We discussed confidentiality and signed release forms. Out of respect for privacy I did not use anyone's actual name in the case studies placed in the beginning of each chapter. I hoped to simply allow the energy and passion of their experiences to be given a safe place to be retold. If testimony is how many find their ways to the good news, then each person interviewed brought me closer to an unconditionally Loving Creator, as they all said, let's tell others a story that may help other people like themselves; it was empathy in its purest form.

By combining points of view, I attempted to allow us all to hear how multiple people are growing, and are challenged. It was always written from the view of my deepest core beliefs that we are all good-hearted, and well-intentioned, people who are simply trying (and sometimes failing) in their attempts to have rewarding relationships with family members. I hope my work has assumed that we are all doing the best we can, with what we have been given. May this writing also embody the concept, often quoted by Maya Angelou, that "when we know better we do better."

We Don't Know What We Don't Know, Until We Do

It was by receiving courage from the quote, "Despite how open, peaceful, and loving you attempt to be, people can only meet you as deeply as they've met themselves," that I hit the "send" button on this book. That quote pushed me to forgive myself, and not be concerned with being perfect. That said, I deeply apologize for where any of my own unmet insecurities have been brought into this story. I ask your forgiveness for what I do not yet know, and "what I don't know that I don't know." That said, any mistakes leading us to empathy, or a renewed ability to see the "other" person in the room, I must therefore give full honor to the people who allowed me into their lives. May our word "family" always be used as both a noun and a verb: As a person, a place, and a thing for us all to celebrate, explore, and adore.

'Perfect Love Drives Away Fear'

In the creation of this book, I had to examine my own fears about living practical theology as my foundation. I was, and still am, absolutely terrified about writing *Living with Momma*. This terror is not just one fear, but a cluster of little fears, scattered throughout these pages. I am saying out loud some tough questions I have asked myself over the years. Being absolutely open about my own doubts concerning *if* our lives actually do give power and agency to the Holy Spirit and *if* we are given fruit, why is it in increasing measure? These can be challenging questions for any pastor to explain, to say the least.

That has led to the paradox I am writing from, where I am both asking "can we really," while at the same time (pro)claiming, "sure, we can." I am receiving comfort from being created in the image of a loving God (betzelem Elohim), and understanding that most things spiritual come with more questions than answers. Once, not many years ago, my own mind, and heart, were boxed in, forcing what is Holy into something that resembled a church building, *instead of something unmeasurable.* I owe credit to my beginning to see the beauty of *LIVING* within the paradoxes towards my sandwich clan, the compassionate listeners in a circle of trust, and my very patient professors at Columbia. I became excited when searching for my own hidden wholeness as described by Thomas Merton, who said our wholeness "lies beneath the broken surface of our lives," and from Parker Palmer, who is still helping me see that I could feel whole again, because I AM.

That said, I pray, in these huge claims of spiritual gifts, where it is important to see what is *not* listed in scripture concerning the gifts of the Spirit (Gal. 5). What is *not* listed are powerful signs, wonders, and the trappings of religious resumés. I have known some who have claimed there is "evidence" of fruit, and with great hubris they call it "signs of faith." Sadly, most people I have met, who say that it is okay to use human forms of measurement concerning spiritual gifts, have gone on to harm (unintentionally or not) many young learners' hearts. People who were eager to show they were fruitful, and thus faithful, often become trapped (as I once was) in the dogma of religion that throws tons of fertilizer on the "do's" and "do not do's" of scripture. So to be clear, I pray this book never makes claims that "measuring growth" and "pruning of vines" are specific ways for anyone to be measuring our fruits.

'You Will Know Them by Their Fruit'

Divine fruit is like manna from heaven. Manna was nourishment collected daily for survival in the desert (Exodus 16:1-36). I claim that spiritual nourishment needs to be gathered daily otherwise it will spoil. Why? Maybe if it didn't, we would try to make it a commodity to sell or trade. We would use it to say we are better and we have more than you so you need us to provide, which would take the Creator out of the actual equation. Maybe it is because we are then reminded where our spiritual selves can rest in this commercially driven society. Maybe it is because we are reminded that we are taken care of by a compassionate Creator every day.

For former spiritual slaves like me, learning to trust my needs will be met by a Creator I cannot physically see, will probably take much wandering around in the heat before I can understand many of the fundamental truths about Love. Honestly, it takes a conscious effort to not limit a beautiful analogy—like a parable—which is illustrating being fruitful by fitting it literally into our limited human life. What is the point of being made in the image of what is unmeasurable? Maybe, this is the point. Our soul's continued yearning for the ability to walk with our physical self and our divine self *together,* in the cool of a garden made "very good" just for us.

Another cluster of fear is spoken when I claim that a person can hear and see and walk in places that are spiritual. I fear it will sound like a challenge to orthodoxy or tradition when it is not. Spiritual thinking is bigger than religious tradition. For example: There are people who have prayed (myself included) to surrender ourselves to the Creator fully, as

Christ did on the cross. While the sentiment may at first seem noble, no one in twenty-first–century America has ever literally been tortured and hung on a cross *for the sins of others*. Only Jesus did that and we don't have to because he did. So, that prayer seems rather childish and emotionally contrived to me, now.

What seems to be a more risky and devoted type of prayer in twenty-first–century America is to be willing to surrender all my childish concepts of "what love is" back to an unconditionally Loving Creator. To ask, "Please help me to surrender to being more loving, peaceful, patient, kind, gentle, joyful, faithful, good, and self-controlled to what *is* perfectly lovingly and endlessly divine…" Now *that* is a prayer where someone in the twenty-first century could *actually* have to show actions behind intent. It is a prayer where our actions may, or may not, allow the broken thoughts and tender moments in our lives to be strengthened and healed in our innermost being (Eph. 3:16).

Spiritual Healing Takes Time

Another cluster of fear is spoken when I say spiritual healing takes time. Just like an apple or a peach tree doesn't just show up automatically, fully grown. So too is the fruit of the Spirit. Because it is divine, *it is made complete*, but it still grows in ever-increasing measure. Such is the paradox of a divine gift: It is not one gift at all. In our twenty-first–century American culture, we are not usually known for being patient in our pursuit of growth. Being in a space of ever-increasing measure takes time and patience. *How do we live patiently with a gift that a divine? How can our caregiving Spirit keep handing us fruit if we do not pick and fill up on it? How is choosing to believe that patiently waiting- while we are growing- a way to be "sure of what we hope for and certain of what we cannot see"? Is there a space where the divine and the human selves can meet more than a concept?* I walk in that space most days and the adventure is one of LIVING fruitfully in ever increasing measure. Still, since there are those days where uncontrollable life events snatch me right out of anything that remotely resembles a peaceful self, I must remember spiritual healing takes time and I need to be willing to make a plan for some extra self care.

My most obvious cluster of fear (to me anyway) is that I claim to be *LIVING* a Good Life by picking fruit with the hand of a practical theologian. What I have been talking about is a very new practice for me, even though I have a master's degree in theology. When reading through scriptures, we can see that the Corinthian and Galatian churches took pleasure in their gifts, but they also saw that the gifts' importance is not held with stems and branches attaching them to us, but are found in both their temporal and ever-increasing abilities to be with, in, for, and from Love *all at the same time*. For me, what that looks like is this: Since I was once spiritually broken by life events fractured by legalism, for me to be *willing* to interact with ancient texts and scriptures *is my way* towards faith- that I am choosing to act in a loving manner toward my Creator. I am always learning to trust that God and church are two different things and I can no longer live well or healthy spiritually by blaming mistakes of humans on a divine Spirit.

Thus by offering and answering tough practical questions about my actual life, I have been gifted with seeing wide-open spaces I never knew existed in Holy scriptures. By feeding on the divine fruit, I can hope again in a power called the Creator, and also give agency to a Holy Spirit within me. By using practical theology, I claim to find comfort from being created in the image of God (betzelem Elohim). I no longer try to box in what is Universally Holy and unmeasurably loving.

So, if you have made it this far in the book, a warm welcome is now being extended to you—as a new member of the sandwich clan. We are just a group of learners who want to be *LIVING* with our families in homes that are full of love, joy, peace, patience, kindness, goodness, gentleness and self-control, in ever-increasing measure. Here. Take and eat some well-ripened fruit offered by other members of our tribe. Feel free to connect with us at our www.livingwithmomma.com page. May we all continue to enjoy the benefits of a journey, in a very good garden, where our human selves hang out with all that is Divine around us.

Bibliography

Anderson, Keith R. *Reading Your Life's Story: An Invitation to Spiritual Mentoring.* Downers Grove, IL: InterVarsity Press, 2016.

Armstrong, Karen. *The Great Transformation: The Beginning of Our Religious Traditions.* New York: Random House, 2007.

Armstrong, Karen. *Twelve Steps to a Compassionate Life.* New York: Anchor Press, 2010.

Bradshaw, John. *Healing the Shame that Binds You.* Deerfield, FL: Health Press, 2005.

Brown, Brené. *Braving the Wilderness: The Quest for True Belonging and the Courage to Stand Alone.* New York: Random House, 2017.

Brown, Brené. *The Gifts of Imperfection: Let Go of Who You Think You Are Supposed to Be and Embrace Who You Are.* New York: Hazelden Publishing, 2010.

Brown, William. *Transitions: Making Sense of Life's Changes.* Cambridge, MA: Da Capo Press, 2004.

Coleman, Joshua. *When Parents Hurt: Compassionate Strategies When You and Your Grown Child Don't Get Along.* New York: Harper Collins, 2008.

Bstan-'dzin-rgya-mtsho, Dalai Lama XIV, Desmond Tutu, and Douglas Carlton Abrams. *The Book of Joy: Lasting Happiness in a Changing World.* New York: Avery, 2016.

Davenport, Barrie. *Peace of Mindfulness: Everyday Rituals to Conquer Anxiety and Claim Unlimited Inner Peace.* Bold Living Press, 2014.

Miller-McLemore, Bonnie J. *The Wiley Blackwell Companion to Practical Theology.* West Sussex, UK: Blackwell, 2014.

Osmer, Richard R. *Practical Theology: An Introduction.* Grand Rapids, MI: Eerdmans, 2008.

Palmer, Parker J. *A Hidden Wholeness: A Journey Toward an Undivided Life.* San Francisco, CA: Jossey-Bass, 2004.

Rohr, Richard R., and Andres Ebert. *The Enneagram: A Christian Perspective.* New York: Crossroads, 2013.

Rohr, Richard et al. *Contemplation in Action: This Is What Yahweh Asks of You.* New York: Crossroads, 2006.

Web Resources

General Elder Care Resources

American Association of Retired Persons. https://www.aarp.org

A Place for Mom. https://www.aplaceformom.com

Elder Care Online. http://www.ec-online.net

Family Caregiver Alliance. https://www.caregiver.org

Hospice Foundation of America. http://www.hospicefoundation.org

National Alliance for Caregiving. http://www.caregiving.org

Government Resources

Alzheimer's information. http://www.alzheimers.gov

Eldercare Directory. https://www.eldercaredirectory.org/state-resources.
htm

Eldercare Locator. http://www.eldercare.gov

Government Benefits, Grants, and Loans. https://www.usa.gov/
benefits-grants-loans

Long-term Care. http://www.longtermcare.gov

Articles, Blogs, and Compassionate Paths to Explore

Senior Living Blog. http://www.aplaceformom.com/blog

Eisner Foundation. http://eisnerfoundation.org

Leah Eskenazi, "How to hire in-home help when your aging parents don't want to move," PBS NewsHour, November 7, 2014, Long-Term Care, https://www.pbs.org/newshour/health/dont-want-move-hiring-home-help

Sven Mawson, "The Elderly: Where Should We Put Them, and Who Should Pay?," Ethics of Development in a Global Environment, June 4, 1999, https://web.stanford.edu/class/e297c/poverty_prejudice/soc_sec/elderly.htm

Programs of All-Inclusive Care for the Elderly (PACE). https://www.medicare.gov/your-medicare-costs/help-paying-costs/pace/pace.html

LiveStrong.com. https://www.livestrong.com

Living with Momma (web companion to this book). www.livingwithmomma.com

World Peace Project. www.Adamswpp.com

Glossary

Assisted Living

A community designed for seniors who are no longer able to live on their own safely, but who do not require the higher level of care provided in a nursing home. Assistance with medications, activities, meals, and housekeeping are provided.

See also: Independent living; Nursing home; Retirement community

Caregiver Self

The soulful side of a person's self that challenges the concepts that people are fixed and unchanging beings, but are instead beings who are created for the "AHA!" moments in life.

Caretaker Self

Someone who supports a person, an animal, or someone's property with physical and emotional general upkeep.

Baby Boomer

A person who was born between the years 1946 and 1964. The first baby boomers turned sixty-five in 2011, and the last will turn sixty-five in 2029. By 2030, baby boomers over sixty-five years of age will make up 20 percent of the U.S. population.

Boomerang Generation

Generally applies to young adults who share a home with their parents after previously living on their own—thus boomeranging back to the home residence.

Empty Nester

A parent whose children have grown up and moved away from home.

Formal Caregivers

Paid care providers who provide care in the home or in a care setting (such as a day care facility, residential facility, or long-term care facility).

Generation X

A person born (roughly) between the years 1965 and 1984.

Generation Y

A person born anywhere from the mid-1970s to the mid-2000s. (FYI: This is not a commonly used term. The existence of this distinct generation is being debated by sociologists and Pew Research Center.)

Independent Living

A living arrangement in a community where older residents can lead active lives and have friends their own age to socialize with. Typically, residents own or rent an apartment or home and the responsibilities of physically caring for a home are alleviated by the community.

Informal Caregiver

An unpaid individual (for example, a spouse, partner, family member, friend, or neighbor) involved in assisting another person with activities of daily living and/or medical tasks.

Millennial

According to the U.S. Census Bureau, a person born between the years 1982 and 2000.

Nursing Home

A facility that provides nursing care and houses a population that requires around-the-clock care and monitoring. Typically, specialty nursing care, physical and speech therapy, and physician care are provided. *See also:* Assisted Living; Independent Living; Retirement Community.

Retirement Community

A community designed exclusively for older adults to live independently. Typically, most residents own their own homes and enjoy provided community activities. Home care agencies can provide some care when needed.

See also: Independent Living

Sandwich Generation

People who live their lives providing care for both aging parents and adult children.

About the Author

Elizabeth B. Adams is the founder of The World Peace Project, LLC, and the creator of the L.I.V.I.N.G. program. She helps people (re)discover rewarding relationships with their families, neighbors, and faith communities.

She is the author of *Living With Momma: A Guide to Caring for Adult Children, Aging Parents and Ourselves.*

She has a master's degree in theology from Columbia Theological Seminary (2014) and bachelor's degrees in cultural anthropology, sociology, and religious studies from Agnes Scott College (2011). She is an ordained minister in the National Christian Churches of America. As a pastoral caregiver and researcher, she helps to (re)define outdated or traditional family roles into fulfilling twenty-first–century relationships.

She is an accomplished speaker and has presented to audiences around the United States on issues within multi-generational relationships, international adoption, and inter-faith issues.

She and her husband raised three daughters, who have all boomeranged in and out as adult children. For now, she and her husband live in an empty nest with a golden retriever, a rescue dog, and an African grey parrot who thinks she owns the house.

http://www.livingwithmomma.com

http://www.Elizabeth@AdamsWPP.com

http://fb.me/ElizabethBAdamsAuthor

Acknowledgments

To the Morgan James Publishing team: Special thanks to David Hancock, CEO & Founder for believing in me and my message. To my Author Relations Manager, Margo Toulouse, thanks for making the process seamless and easy. Many more thanks to everyone else, but especially Jim Howard, Bethany Marshall, and Nicole Watkins.

Also, my most heartfelt thanks to family and friends who gave suggestions on the many drafts it took to make this book. A BIG love you goes to my favorite editor and oldest daughter: Indya Furlong. Your walking this adventure with me gave me courage to keep celebrating, exploring, and adoring all that is beautiful in our family garden.

Thank You

Thanks for reading!

I'd love to hear about your fruitful adventures in *Living with Momma: A Guide to Caring for Aging Parents, Adult Children, and Ourselves.* Please email me or comment on the World Peace Project Facebook page at http://fb.me/ElizabethBAdamsAuthor.

If you are interested in exploring further within your Caring Self email me at the World Peace Project website http://www.Elizabeth@AdamsWPP.com for the dates of upcoming retreats, workshops, and video chats.

To support you in your journey I have created free u-tube video's to help you shift away from your old stories while guiding you through the (re)writing of your new rewarding relationships with your family. As a way of saying thank you for your purchase, I am also offering a free companion website that is exclusive to readers of Living with Momma. With the companion website, you can have access to a collection of printable guides, checklists, questions and resources.

>> Go here to access Living With Momma companion website<<
www.livingwithmomma.com

Contribution Pledge

"The marvelous vision of the peaceable Kingdom, in which all violence has been overcome and all men, women, and children live in loving unity ... [is seen] every time we show compassion to a suffering person ... we are making the vision come true. Instead of making us escape real life, this beautiful vision gets us involved."
– Center for Action and Contemplation

At least 670,000 Americans were homeless in 2016. Even more shocking is that over 35 percent of these people had young children with them at the time.

As a former pastor providing services to Atlanta's homeless community, I met many amazing, hardworking people who were knocked off their feet by a sudden crisis. For reasons too many to name here, they did not have family to help them. This calling taught me many things but mainly that homelessness can affect anybody, including middle-class Americans.

Therefore, I pledge a percentage of all book sales from the *Living with Momma* series to communities that are working to prevent and end homelessness in America. For a list of preselected communities, please visit me at www.livingwithmomma.com.

Morgan James makes all of our titles available
through the Library for All Charity Organization.

www.LibraryForAll.org

CPSIA information can be obtained
at www.ICGtesting.com
Printed in the USA
BVHW081044110319
542321BV00001B/89/P

9 781642 791471